Parenting from the Heart

Parenting from the Heart is a fresh, accessible, authoritative pocket book for helping your gifted, bright, or creative child become resilient and psychologically vibrant, both in and out of the classroom!

Engaging chapters explore how to support your child's social-emotional development through teaching, reinforcing, and modeling the author's research-based framework, "strengths of the heart," championing the dynamic trio of Emotional Intelligence, social skills, and character strengths. Featuring diverse, illustrative examples, effective interventions, and frequently asked questions to help you put concepts into practice, this book offers essential information for raising and supporting responsible, caring, empathic, and resilient gifted children.

This book is a must-read for all caregivers seeking to get ahead of potential behavioral, academic, and social challenges while building a healthy foundation to become a calm, reflective, and thoughtful parent.

Steven I. Pfeiffer is a licensed and nationally board-certified psychologist, author, speaker, and consultant. Dr. Pfeiffer is Emeritus Professor at Florida State University and previously served as Professor and Director of Duke University's gifted program. He is considered one of the leading authorities on the social-emotional world of gifted kids.

Parenting from the Heart

Raising Resilient and Successful Smart Kids

Steven I. Pfeiffer

Routledge
Taylor & Francis Group

NEW YORK AND LONDON

Designed cover image: © Getty Images

First published 2024
by Routledge
605 Third Avenue, New York, NY 10158

and by Routledge
4 Park Square, Milton Park, Abingdon, Oxon, OX14 4RN

Routledge is an imprint of the Taylor & Francis Group, an informa business

© 2024 Steven I. Pfeiffer

Library of Congress Cataloging-in-Publication Data
Names: Pfeiffer, Steven I., author.
Title: Parenting from the heart : raising resilient and
successful smart kids / Steven I. Pfeiffer.
Description: New York, NY : Routledge, 2024. |
Includes bibliographical references. |
Summary: – Provided by publisher.
Identifiers: LCCN 2023006523 (print) | LCCN 2023006524 (ebook) |
ISBN 9781032262048 (paperback) | ISBN 9781003287070 (ebook)
Subjects: LCSH: Gifted children–Psychology. |
Gifted children–Mental health. | Parenting.
Classification: LCC HQ773.5 .P45 2024 (print) |
LCC HQ773.5 (ebook) | DDC 649/.15–dc23/eng/20230224
LC record available at https://lccn.loc.gov/2023006523
LC ebook record available at https://lccn.loc.gov/2023006524

ISBN: 978-1-032-26204-8 (pbk)
ISBN: 978-1-003-28707-0 (ebk)

DOI: 10.4324/9781003287070

Typeset in Palatino
by Newgen Publishing UK

Contents

Preface

John Steinbeck reportedly said that you write for one single reader. He opined that he found it helpful to pick out one person—a real person you know or an imagined one and write to that one person. With all due respect for John Steinbeck, I have taken a slightly different tack.

This book is written for not one, but for every parent (or grandparent or guardian) interested in learning more about raising well-adjusted, resilient, optimistic, and successful kids. Teachers who work with the gifted may also find this pocketbook informative.

The pocketbook introduces a "triple package" of traits—Emotional Intelligence, social skills, and character strengths, called "strengths of the heart"—which predict to successful life outcomes for gifted kids.

Special appreciation at the start to psychiatrist and Holocaust survivor Viktor Frankl, who reminds us, "When we are no longer able to change a situation, we are challenged to change ourselves" (2006).

Reference

Frankl, Viktor (2006). *Man's search for meaning*. Boston, MA: Beacon Press.

Acknowledgments

This book was conceived and written with great appreciation and abundant love for my wife, Jan, and my three children, Andrea, Kevin, and Leslie. This book was also written with my five grandchildren in mind; Jayda, Kayden, Maya, Shiloh, and Thai. You each have taught me so much about child development, individual differences, parenting, patience, forbearance, moderation, and serenity.

Finally, this book is dedicated with immense respect for the many hundreds of parents, families, and gifted children and adolescents that I've had the great privilege and honor of working with over the last 45 years in my practice as a psychologist. My hope in writing this pocket-sized book is that what I've learned over the course of my career during counseling sessions and parent workshops resonates as relevant lessons to the readers of this book.

I was taught early in my clinical training as a family therapist at Philadelphia Child Guidance Center to give a "gift" to your client in each session. The metaphor of a gift might be a compliment, insight, praise, support for a suggestion that the client proposed, or a metaphor, image, or even personal disclosure that helps the client clarify a difficult issue or topic discussed during the therapy session. In this same spirit, I dedicate this book as my gift to every parent committed to raising resilient, optimistic, thoughtful, and considerate gifted kids. To encouraging strengths of the heart!

1

The Search for Optimal Mental Health

Successful Parenting

One quiet, sunny afternoon, I was sitting in my office overlooking the bustling campus grounds of Duke University, a beautiful, bucolic, and highly respected university located in North Carolina. I was adjusting to my very first summer as Executive Director of the Duke program for gifted students, Duke TIP.[1] While preparing for a budget meeting with my boss, Duke's Associate Provost, a loud knock on my office door brought me out of my reverie. The director of Duke TIPs education programs, a typically calm, unruffled, and seasoned educator, insisted that I take five minutes away from prepping for my annual budget meeting to talk with a summer residential student—who we affectionately called TIPsters. Apparently, the student, Claudio,[2] had found himself embroiled in a heated and

DOI: 10.4324/9781003287070-1

rather nasty argument with a few of his fellow classmates, a disagreeable-enough classroom conflict to warrant the student being asked to leave the classroom and brought to deal with me. In my role as headmaster of Duke's summer program, and as a trained psychologist, staff found me a helpful resource in dealing with students on campus who were challenging—challenging behaviorally, academically, socially, or emotionally.

This bright young man—just shy of his 15th birthday, sat across from me with an angry, brooding scowl. He was in no mood to acknowledge, much less discuss, what had triggered his frightful mood. It didn't take a Scotland Yard detective to see that he was neither inclined to talk about nor explore with me why he was unable to keep his cool during a heated classroom discussion. This incident (early in my tenure at Duke, back in the summer of 1998) of an intellectually gifted young man acting rather dumb—totally losing his cool and melting down to the point where he was unable to manage his emotions under the pressure of a spirited classroom discussion—became a watershed moment in my work with bright kids. It was an epiphany for me. The incident with this student prompted a recognition of my need to better understand the social and emotional world of gifted students (Pfeiffer, 2013a, b; 2017; 2018).

The epiphany that I came to recognize, almost 30 years ago, was that a great many fabulously bright students—intellectually gifted kids—with magnificent *"head strengths,"* didn't always have nearly as well-developed *"heart strengths."* By heart strengths, I mean skills, personal assets, attitudes, and values in the areas of self-awareness, social maturity, open-mindedness, self-management, honesty, gratitude, agreeableness, kindness, empathy, humility, compassion, self-reflection, tact, and forgiveness. And responsible decision-making. I came to view these character strengths, virtues, skills, and competencies as *"strengths of the heart."*

This little pocketbook explores my journey, over the course of my career, discovering the importance and relevance of *strengths of the heart* in the lives of gifted kids, adolescents, and young adults (Pfeiffer, 2018). The pocketbook describes how parents can help their kids become better adjusted, more happy, thoughtful, self-reliant, and optimistic. And more resilient. I am excited to share this story with you, the reader.

For a short moment back to Claudio's story. Claudio was fantastically bright, by any measure of intelligence. In the fourth grade, his tested IQ score on a popular and widely used test of intellectual ability was above 140. In the sixth grade, he took the SAT college admissions exam—a test originally designed for high school juniors and seniors, in a procedure for younger students that is called by talent search programs "out of level testing." He scored in the 99th percentile for sixth graders. A bright young man, indeed. However, his instructors and the residential staff quickly recognized during his summer on the campus of Duke University that this young adolescent was not very emotionally intelligent!

He often behaved in a self-centered and egotistical manner. According to staff, he would lose control of his emotions, and make bad decisions, especially under stress when in the classroom, dorm, or cafeteria. He seemed to have little appreciation or concern for how his behavior impacted others. He lacked several important social skills expected of kids his age, such as waiting his turn, listening before responding, accepting diverse opinions, and sharing with others. And yet, he was a super-bright kid. He had amazing head strengths!

Claudio didn't have a psychiatric disorder. He wasn't a gifted kid with a co-existing psychological disorder. What we call the twice exceptional or 2e student (see Pfeiffer & Foley Nicpon, 2018). It would have been much less complicated for our summer academy to view and "pigeon-hole" him, and many other bright students like him, as twice exceptional or 2e. But that really wasn't his issue. Claudio was an intellectually bright young man. But he lacked a commensurate level of *social intelligence*. This was his personal demon causing him a great many small and large problems! He could be quirky. For sure. But he wasn't twice exceptional. He didn't have a psychiatric disorder. He didn't have a sub-clinical disorder, either (Pfeiffer, 2013b; Post, 2022). He was super bright; he had abundant *head strengths*. However, Claudio was lacking in commensurate social intelligence, Emotional Intelligence, and *social skills*; what I call *heart strengths* (Pfeiffer et al., 2016). In subsequent chapters you will learn more about *heart strengths*.

This pocketbook introduces why *heart strengths* make a real difference in your son or daughter's life. The pocketbook talks about ways that you, as a parent, can help teach, encourage, and reinforce these important life skills. These are life skills that build resilience and protect your child from the many challenges that all kids face growing up. Helping your child develop *heart strengths* will contribute to their well-being, resilience, and life success. And actually optimize their mental health. Parents can, and do, make a real difference in the success that their bright kids experience growing up by encouraging *heart strengths*. I am confident that the lessons provided in this easy-to-read pocketbook will inspire and work for you.

I hope that you have the motivation and patience to travel with me on this journey to learn more about how to nurture *strengths of the heart*. In my experience as a therapist, consultant, speaker, and teacher, *strengths of the heart* make a real difference in the lives of bright kids like your child. In subsequent chapters, you will read about why, and how to teach and encourage *heart strengths* such as empathy, compassion, gratitude, persistence, patience, grit, and humility. In my clinical practice, in our research lab (for example, Pfeiffer et al., 2016) and in others' investigations (Dweck, 2016; Seligman, 2011: Siegel & Hartzell, 2016), the *heart strengths* and life skills that are explored in this pocketbook have been shown to promote resilience, well-being, and life satisfaction. These ideas are backed by solid scientific research.

I think that you will find it enjoyable and easy to implement the strategies and ideas in this book into your own family life. And I am confident that you will agree with the proposition that encouraging *heart strengths*, along with *head strengths*, makes perfectly good sense.

As I write this book, children's mental health is in crisis. Prior to the Covid-19 crisis, for example, the Centers for Disease Control and Prevention (CDC) reported that one in five children have a mental disorder (www.cdc. gov/gov/childrensmentalhealth/access.html). Most mental health authorities assume that recent pandemic-related stressors have only further increased the unique challenges that kids today face (APA, 2022), compromising kids' ability to cope and be resilient. A great many children and youth today suffer from social, emotional, and behavioral challenges that don't necessarily qualify as mental disorders—counselors call these subclinical problems. They aren't mental health disorders. But these behaviors, nonetheless, can be distressful for the child and certainly unsettling and worrisome for the parents. And they compromise the child's success trajectory.

One of my favorite opinion writers, David Brooks, penned a piece in *The New York Times*, "America is Falling Apart at the Seams." In this provocative essay, Mr. Brooks points out that all kinds of bad behavior are now on the rise. As two examples, he cites a *Wall Street Journal* report that schools have seen an increase in both minor incidents and more serious issues, such as fights and gun possession, and a rising drug epidemic that just keeps getting worse. He concludes his essay by suggesting that perhaps some kind of social, spiritual, or moral virus may be at the core of the impolite, coarse, and disrespectful, boorish, selfish, and self-centered behaviors seen in the USA and worldwide (Brooks, 2022). Brooks intimates that perhaps our nation has stumbled into a dangerous period of narcissism.

I contend that, whether Mr. Brooks' thesis is correct or not, putting *strengths of the heart* at the forefront of what we teach in our homes as parents (and in schools, but that's a topic for another book!) is the perfect antidote for many of today's mental health, spiritual, and moral ills. I think that you will agree after reading this book. I hope so!

I have tried to write this book in a parent-friendly, nonacademic style. I have avoided using jargon and unfamiliar psychological terms. However, it was impossible to completely eliminate all psychological or scholarly terms. You will encounter the following terms in the book. Many also appear in the gifted literature. I thought that you would find it helpful to have this glossary or wordlist to refer to if you aren't familiar with any of these terms.

Glossary of Terms Found in This Book and in the Gifted Literature

Asperger syndrome. Asperger syndrome or Asperger's is a neurodevelopmental disorder characterized by significant difficulties in social interaction and nonverbal communication. It is often accompanied by restricted and repetitive patterns of behavior and interests. Recently, the medical profession has categorized Asperger's as a subtype and "on the spectrum" of autism spectrum disorder, not a unique diagnostic condition. However, many still refer to gifted kids who have Asperger's. Asperger's is marked by relatively unimpaired intelligence and language. The cause of Asperger's is not well understood, although it is considered a largely inherited or genetic disorder. In the author's experience, many persons with high IQ have been labeled as "neurodiverse" or having Asperger's—a type of twice exceptionality or 2e. Many intellectually bright clients have come to my practice with the diagnosis of gifted *and* Asperger's—twice exceptional or 2e. However, I have come to view many of these fascinating kids as, what I call, "gifted and behaviorally quirky" but *not* necessarily having a psychiatric or medical disability which would qualify them as twice exceptional. This is *not* an insignificant distinction. All too often, professionals and parents alike are quick to label quirky behaviors as abnormal. Some persons diagnosed with Asperger's—and those on the autism spectrum—have a deficit in appreciating that another person's mental state might be different from their own—that the other person's thinking, beliefs, desires, intentions, or emotions might not exactly mirror their own. Also see **Theory of mind**.

Character strengths. *Character strengths* are one of the three components of my *strengths of the heart* model. The other two are *social skills* and *Emotional Intelligence*. Character strengths (and virtues) are considered beneficial and worthy by almost all cultures and societies, throughout history, in both the West and East. Many in the positive psychology camp theorize that there are universal *character strengths* and virtues, such as humility, spirituality, prudence, forgiveness, love, kindness, integrity, and bravery. Christopher Peterson and Martin Seligman, pioneers in the positive psychology camp, presented a theoretical framework and research in support of 24 universal and measurable character strengths in their book, *Character Strengths and Virtues* (2004).

Compassion. Compassion is first cousin to empathy. They are not the same thing, but they certainly are related. Empathy depicts knowing how another person feels and even what they might be thinking. Empathy can also describe when you physically feel what another person feels, as though their emotions were contagious or transmittable. This type of emotional infection depends on cells in the brain called mirror neurons. More on this in Chapter 4. When empathy moves us to act to resolve a person's predicament or suffering, we are demonstrating compassion. Compassion can range from the most elementary to the most exceptional and heroic, according to renowned psychologist Paul Ekman, and even the Dalai Lama.

Emotional Intelligence. Quite simply, *Emotional Intelligence* or *EI*, as it is often called, is a person's ability to perceive or "read," understand, manage, and handle emotions and emotionally charged situations. As you will read in Chapter 4, *EI* is one of three components of my strengths of the heart model. The other two are *character strengths* and *social skills.* Researchers and mental health practitioners believe that people with higher *EI* are better able to recognize their own emotions and those of others, adjust their emotions to adapt to different situations, and discern among different emotions and label them more accurately.

Empathy. Empathy is the ability to sense or correctly "read" other people's emotions and feelings. It includes the ability to imagine what another person might be thinking or feeling. Emotion researchers differentiate between at least two types of empathy: "affective empathy" and "cognitive empathy (also called "perspective taking"). Empathy has deep roots in our evolutionary history; there is growing evidence of a genetic basis for empathy. I like to think of empathy and compassion as first cousins—related but not exactly the same.

Flow. Being "in the zone" is the mental experience that describes the flow state. Essentially, flow is the mental state when a person is performing some challenging activity and is fully immersed or absorbed in a feeling of heightened attention and energized focus. One's sense of time actually is transformed when in a flow state. The flow concept is widely recognized across a variety of fields, including science, the performing and graphic arts, sports and athletics, and creative writing. In writing this book—which was a labor of love, on occasion—I almost unconsciously slipped into a flow state and lost all sense of time. The reader may also have experienced flow or "being in the zone." Some theorists contend that a person's most creative and productive peak accomplishments occur during periods of flow state (see Csikszentmihalyi, 1997).

Gifted. A book could be written on what the term "gifted" means. In fact, a great many books have been written on this very topic. I have written two such books: *Essentials* *of Gifted Assessment* (Wiley, 2015) and *Serving the Gifted* (Routledge, 2013). A clever, easy read on giftedness is Linda Silverman's, *Giftedness 101* (2013). Another friendly read is Gail Post's *The Gifted Parenting Journey* (2022). My personal view is that gifted kids are individuals who demonstrate outstanding performance or evidence of potential for outstanding performance, when compared to other kids of the same age, experience, and opportunity in a culturally valued field or domain. Such as academics, the performing arts, drawing, painting, or sculpture, writing, athletics, and leadership ability. The gifted tend to have a thirst to excel in one or more academic domains. And they almost always benefit from special programs, services, or resources that align with their unique innate abilities (Neihart, Pfeiffer, & Cross, 2015). Many, but not all, gifted are creative, and some, but not all, have multiple gifts (Pfeiffer & Jarosewich, 2023). The gifted child's environment is a critical factor that influences how far their giftedness will develop. Some authorities argue that giftedness should not be viewed from a high achievement perspective but rather viewed as an inner experience to be nurtured holistically (Silverman, 2013). This view contends that a great many if not all gifted are intense, sensitive, perfectionistic, keenly perceptive, asynchronous with uneven development, and often marginalized and misunderstood (Post, 2022; Zakoian, 2020). Bottom line: An IQ score of 130 or higher remains the most accepted cut-off for giftedness.

Grit. Positive psychology considers grit a noncognitive trait, an enduring characteristic of the individual. Grit describes a powerful motivational state and consists of two components: a person's *perseverance* and also their *passion* for a particular activity or event. William James first talked about this trait back in 1907 in a classic article that appeared in *Science*. Most recently, Angela Duckworth brought new attention to the concept of grit in her research and admired writings (Duckworth, 2016). Grit has become a popular concept in competitive athletics, in the corporate world, and even in the talent development field. Grit is another way of understanding resilience, tenacity, hardiness, ambition, and conscientiousness. Whatever we call it, grit is obviously something parents want their kids to have plenty of!

Intelligence. Intelligence is a multifaceted psychological construct. Most authorities agree that intelligence encompasses the capacity for abstract reasoning, logic, memory, planning ability, problem-solving, mental processing speed, self-awareness, critical and abstract thinking, and even creativity. There are many different definitions and theories. For example, Howard Gardner popularized the notion of "multiple intelligences" (Gardner, 1993). We know that individuals differ from one another in their ability to understand complex ideas, adapt effectively and efficiently to challenges in the environment, and overcome obstacles using problem-solving—intelligence. As the reader is probably aware, there are several tests that measure intelligence. In fact, I authored a rating scale used in gifted identification, the *GRS*™ *2*, published by MHS Assessments. The *GRS*™ *2* is widely used in the USA and globally in gifted identification. The *GRS*™ *2* includes a scale of Intelligence, with forms rated by teachers and parents (Pfeiffer & Jarosewich, 2003; 2023). Also see **Gifted**. Recent research has identified evidence for a relationship between personality and intelligence. Personality factors that relate to higher intelligence are openness to experience, intellectual engagement, and unconventionality (see Anglim et al., 2022).

Mindset. Mindset is a set of beliefs that influence how we make sense of our world, including how we view ourselves. One's mindset influences how we think, feel, react, plan, and approach challenges. According to Carol Dweck, there are two basic mindsets: fixed and growth. If you embrace a fixed mindset, Dweck argues, then you believe that your abilities are pretty much fixed traits and can't be improved. You might even downplay trying hard or extending grit since you believe that your God-given talents lead to success and can't be improved upon. The mindset theory contends that fixed mindsets are brittle and easy to crumble under stress. On the other hand, a growth mindset is the internal belief that talents and abilities can be increased through hard work, grit, and persistence. Dweck's work on mindset gained traction in the gifted field because some argued that many high IQ kids adopt a fixed mindset, which creates obstructions down the road when they first face highly challenging tasks—and give up.

Neurodiverse. Neurodiversity is a relatively new term; it wasn't around when I was trained early in my career as a psychologist. The term was created in the 1990s by Judy Singer, a sociologist who acknowledges that she apparently is on the autism spectrum herself (Singer, 2017). Neurodivergent means persons who think and learn and process information and act differently from the way most do (referred to as "neurotypical"). Examples of neurodiversity include persons with attention deficit hyperactivity disorder (ADHD), autism spectrum disorder, specific learning disabilities, and Tourette's syndrome. Advocates of the term argue that neurological differences should be respected as a sociological category on a par with gender, race, ethnicity, sexual orientation, or disability status. Professionals and parents alike need to be careful not to over-label everyone who is different as neurodiverse or "on the spectrum." See my cautionary note about the likely overused term, **Asperger's**.

Positive psychology. Positive psychology is a relatively new term in the behavioral sciences. Positive psychology is the scientific study of human flourishing and seeks to understand how we can elevate a person's optimal functioning. Often, writers include the study of virtues, character strengths, and resilience when talking about positive psychology. The concept of positive psychology will be mentioned throughout this pocketbook. Early in my career, I had the good fortune one summer of training with Sir Michael Rutter, MD, renowned British child psychiatrist. Dr. Rutter helped me appreciate the importance, in clinical work with kids and families, of focusing on strengths instead of exclusively working to ameliorate client weaknesses and disorders. His viewpoint on building resilience and focusing on client assets and strengths greatly influenced my own thinking, research, and clinical work.

Quirky behaviors. Quirky is characterized by peculiar, atypical, odd, or unexpected behaviors or qualities. I have come to use the term "quirky" in my clinical practice to describe clients that I have worked with—oftentimes clients who are gifted—who behave in peculiar, eccentric, unconventional, or in odd ways but are *not* necessarily on the autism spectrum. I prefer using the nonmedical term, quirky behaviors, to the more common practice of labeling many kids who shows unusual, atypical, or even weird behaviors as being "neurodiverse" or "on the (autism) spectrum." In my opinion, quirky is less pejorative and less stigmatizing. And it doesn't suggest a faulty neurological basis for quirky behaviors.

Resilience. Resilience is a popular term in developmental psychology and human epidemiology. Resilience research has focused on why some kids and adolescents (and adults) are able to maintain positive adaptation and psychological well-being despite encountering aversive, distressing, stressful, oppressive, and traumatic experiences. Mental health practitioners view resilience as the capacity for successful adaptation despite facing challenging or threatening circumstances—adapting well by mobilizing internal and external resources in the face of adversity, trauma, tragedy, threats, or significant sources of stress. In other words, resilience is the ability to "bounce back" from difficult life experiences and achieve balance, harmony, and positive life outcomes. Resilience at a young age predicts to later positive youth development, and a more positive self-image, greater self-control, higher moral reasoning, and greater social connectedness in adult life. The "take home" conclusion from literally hundreds of resilience research studies is that promoting resilience yields huge benefits for kids and adolescents. This is the reason why I focus this book on resilience! *Heart strengths* and resilience are close relatives in the family tree of subjective well-being and successful life outcomes. Also see **Positive psychology**.

Self-efficacy. Self-efficacy is a person's belief in their ability to act in successful ways necessary to reach specific goals. The goals can be academic, personal, social/interpersonal, spiritual, or vocational. The theory was first proposed by Stanford University professor Albert Bandura (1977). According to Bandura, and later confirmed by many other scientists, self-efficacy influences the actual power that a person can garner when facing difficult challenges. Self-efficacy is highly valued in the behavioral sciences. It is seen as promoting well-being, hardiness, self-confidence, stamina, toughness, grit, and overcoming adversity (resilience). Self-efficacy is a close cousin of grit, internal locus of control, and a growth mindset. Self-efficacy is also related to prosocial behavior. Twin studies have found a heritability factor for self-efficacy, although the genetic research also highlights the role of the family environment in explaining individual differences in self-efficacy (Waaktaar & Torgersen, 2013). Also see **Grit**, **Positive psychology**, and **Resilience**.

Social skills. *Social skills* are used to communicate with others, including verbal, nonverbal, written, and visual. *Social skills* are often referred to as interpersonal skills or *soft skills*. Any time your child interacts with you, another family member, or adult, sibling, or friend, they are using *social skills*—including language, body language, facial expressions, social distancing, and eye contact. Well-developed *social skills* help build and maintain successful peer and adult–child relationships. Poorly developed *social skills*, on the other hand, can hamper your child's social and emotional development, limit their social world, and compromise their well-being and happiness. Savvy *social skills* help gifted kids navigate tricky and challenging social situations. Examples of important *social skills* that I have helped kids develop in my practice include effective communication with others, conflict resolution when disagreements arise, active listening to a person who is communicating with you, relationship management, coping with rejection and disappointment, making a good first impression, taking turns, and speaking kindly and keeping your cool. All too often, very smart kids can lack age-appropriate *social skills* or *people skills* that can create real problems (see Tough, 2012).

Strengths of the heart. *Strengths of the heart*, or *heart strengths*, is a relatively new paradigm or model for thinking about how bright kids with an abundance of *head strengths* can thrive and flourish. When I first conceived *heart strengths*, back in 1998, I proposed that it include how effectively kids managed their feelings and emotions, and how well-developed were their *social skills* and *Emotional Intelligence*. The concept of *heart strengths* is tied to the concepts of risk, vulnerability, stress, and resilience (Allen & Pfeiffer, 1991; Anthony, 1987; Compas, 1987; Garmezy & Rutter, 1983; Pfeiffer, 2017). Philosophically, *heart strengths'* lineage and roots are coupled with positive psychology.

Theory of mind. Theory of mind is a relatively recent concept in psychology first introduced in the 1990s. It refers to a child's capacity to understand other people by ascribing independent mental states to them. Theory of mind denotes that the child understands that another child or adult's mental state may be different from their own. In other words, that another person holds different beliefs, attitudes, desires, intentions, emotions, and ideas. Psychologists recognize that theory of mind is essential for success in everyday social interactions. Deficits in theory of mind implicate the prefrontal cortex and can occur in persons with autism spectrum disorder, ADHD, severe psychiatric disorders such as schizophrenia, and cocaine addiction. Having a theory of mind is similar, but not identical with, the capacity for empathy and compassion. See **Strengths of the Heart** and **Asperger's**.

Twice exceptional. The term twice exceptional, often abbreviated as 2e, refers to gifted or high-ability students who also have some form of disability. The term was introduced to the field in the mid-1990s by educators who recognized that some students in the schools are exceptional because of *both* their giftedness *and* because of their disability—as defined by federal or state eligibility criteria. These disabilities can include specific learning disabilities, speech and language disorders, emotional/behavioral disorders, a physical disability, autism spectrum disorder, difficulties with writing (dysgraphia), sensory processing or integration concerns, and ADHD. Also, see **Asperger's** above. Twice exceptional students often find it difficult in the school environment. Educators are often challenged to successfully differentiate and individualize the classroom learning environment for these special needs students. I have worked with the twice exceptional and have written about this unique population (for example, see Pfeiffer, 2013a; Pfeiffer & Foley-Nicpon, 2018).

Virtues. See **Character strengths** above.

Well-being. The psychological literature on well-being (also called subjective well-being), includes happiness, life satisfaction, and positive affect. Researchers have published papers on how to measure well-being, what contributes to subjective well-being, and different ways to increase this favorable state. Research has looked at how academic and job success and satisfaction, physical health, quality of social contact, amount of activity, and personality contribute to well-being. The most recent thinking is that well-being is a multidimensional construct. Well-being can include both happiness and living a full and deeply satisfying life. Perhaps the most compelling argument for living a life with meaning was proposed by Viktor Frankl in his popular book *Man's Search for Meaning*. In this book, which has sold over 10 million copies and has been translated into 24 languages, Frankl chronicles his experiences as a prisoner in a Nazi concentration camp. I often recommend this beautiful book to parents.

I have intentionally written this small, pocket-size book with a large vision: to provide parents with reader-friendly suggested resources following each chapter that allow the reader to delve more deeply into the topics introduced in the chapter. I hope that readers take time to look at the **Suggested Resources** and **References** following each chapter of this pocket-sized book. For the **Suggested Resources** I have selected nonacademic and easy-to-read resources so that parents can learn more about the "*soft people skills*" that make a real difference in raising successful, well-adjusted, responsible, and resilient kids! Most of these suggested resources are available at neighborhood bookstores and online at www.amazon.com. The **References** section provides a list of the citations found throughout this pocket-size book.

Suggested Resources

Borba, M. (2021). *Thrivers: The surprising reasons why some kids struggle and others shine.* New York: Penguin Random House.

Carnegie, D. (1937). *How to win friends and influence people* (11th printing). New York: Simon and Schuster.

Clarke-Fields, H. (2019). *Raising good humans: A mindful guide to breaking the cycle of reactive parenting and raising kind, confident kids.* Oakland, CA: New Harbinger Publications.

Csikszentmihalyi, M. (1997). *Finding flow: The psychology of engagement with everyday life.* New York: Basic Books.

Frankl, V. (1959). *Man's search for meaning.* Boston, MA: Beacon Press.

Gardner, H. (1993). *Frames of mind: The theory of multiple intelligences.* New York: Basic Books.

Goleman, D. (2006). *Social intelligence: The new science of human relationships.* New York: Bantam Books.

Kennedy-Moore, E., & Lowenthal, M. S. (2011). *Smart parenting for smart kids.* New York: Jossey-Bass.

Leman, K. (2021). *8 secrets to raising successful kids.* Ada, MI: Revell Books.

Nhat Hanh, T. (2009). *Happiness.* Berkeley, CA: Parallax Press.

Seligman, M. E. P. (2011). *Flourish.* New York: Atria Paperback.

Siegel, D. J. (2007). *The mindful brain: Reflection and attunement in the cultivation of wellbeing.* New York: Norton.

Singer, J. (2017). *Neurodiversity: The birth of an idea.* Published by the author.

Zakoian, C. (2020). *Raising gifted children: A practical guide for parents facing big emotions and big potential.* Emeryville, CA: Rockridge Press.

Notes

1 The Duke program for gifted students was launched in 1980, as an initiative of then Duke University Provost William Bevan. Dr. Bevan had visited the Johns Hopkins University Center for Talent Development, an innovative program for gifted pre-collegiate students created by Professor Julian Stanley. The Duke TIP program sadly closed in 2020. I served as Executive Director of the Duke TIP program 1998–2003.

2 In this, and every example throughout the book, I use pseudonyms to protect the anonymity of the students and parents.

References

Allen, J. P., & Pfeiffer, S. I. (1991). Residential treatment of adolescents who do not return to their families. *Child & Adolescent Mental Health Care, 1*, 209–22.

American Psychological Association (APA) (2022). Children's mental health in crisis. *2022 Trends Report* (*Monitor*/2022/01/ Special-Emerging-Trends). Vol. 53 (No. 1), 69.

Anglim, J., Dunlop, P. D., Wee, S., Horwood, S., Wood, J. K., & Marty, A. (2022). Personality and intelligence: A meta-analysis. *Psychological Bulletin, 148* (5–6), 301–336.

Anthony, E. J. (1987). Risk, vulnerability, and resilience: An overview. In E. J. Anthony and B. J. Cohler (Eds.), *The invulnerable child* (pp. 3–48). New York: Guilford Press.

Bandura, A. (1977). Self-efficacy: Toward a unifying theory of behavioral change. *Psychological Review, 84* (2), 191–215.

Brooks, D. (January 13, 2022). America is falling apart at the seams. *The New York Times Opinion Section A*, p. 18. (www. nytimes.com/2022/01/13/opinion/america-falling-apart. html?referringSource=articleShare)

Compas, B. E. (1987). Coping and stress during childhood and adolescence. *Psychological Bulletin, 101*, 393–403.

Csikszentmihalyi, M. (1997). *Finding flow in everyday life.* New York: Basic Books.

Duckworth, A. (2016). *Grit: The power of passion and perseverance.* New York: Scribner.

Dweck, C. S. (2016). The secret of raising smart kids. *Scientific American Mind*, Summer issue, pp. 11–17.

Gardner, H. (1993). *Frames of mind: The theory of multiple intelligences.* New York: Basic Books.

Garmezy, N., & Rutter, M. (Eds.) (1983). *Stress, coping, and development in children.* New York: McGraw-Hill.

Neihart, M., Pfeiffer, S. I., & Cross, T. (2015). What do we know about the social and emotional development of gifted children? In M. Neihart, S. I. Pfeiffer, & T. Cross (Eds.). *The social and emotional development of gifted children: What we know* (2nd Ed.) (pp. 283–297) Waco, TX: Prufrock Press.

Peterson, C., & Seligman, M. E. P. (2004). *Character strengths and virtues: A handbook and classification.* Oxford: Oxford University Press.

Pfeiffer, S. I. (2013a). Lessons learned from working with high-ability students. *Gifted Education International, 29,* 86–97.

Pfeiffer, S. I. (2013b). *Serving the gifted.* New York: Routledge.

Pfeiffer, S. I. (2017). Success in the classroom and in life: Focusing on strengths of the head and strengths of the heart. *Gifted Education International, 33,* 95–101.

Pfeiffer, S. I., & Jarosewich, T. (2003). *Gifted Rating Scales™.* Toronto: MHS Assessments.

Pfeiffer, S. I., & Jarosewich, T. (2023). *Gifted Rating Scales™ 2.* Toronto: MHS Assessments.

Pfeiffer, S. I., Valler, E. C., Burko, J. A., Yarnell, J. B., Branagan, A. M., Smith, S. M., Barbash, E., & Saintil, M. (2016). Focusing on strengths of the heart in understanding success and psychological well-being of high-ability students. *Austin Child and Adolescent Psychiatry, 1,* 1002.

Post, G. (2022). *The gifted parenting journey.* Goshen, KY: Gifted Unlimited.

Seligman, M. E. P. (2011). *Flourish.* New York: Atria Paperback.

Siegel, D. J., & Hartzell, M. (2014). *Parenting from the inside out.* New York: Penguin Group.

Silverman, L. K. (2013). *Giftedness 101.* New York: Springer.

Singer, J. (2017). *Neurodiversity: The birth of an idea.* Published by the author.

Tough, P. (2012). *How children succeed.* New York: Houghton Mifflin Harcourt.

Waaktaar, T., & Torgersen, S. (2013). Self-efficacy is mainly genetic, not learned: A multiple-rater twin study on the causal structure of general self-efficacy in young people. *Twin Research and Human Genetics, 16* (3), 651–660.

Zakoian, C. (2020). *Raising gifted children: A practical guide for parents facing big emotions and big potential.* Emeryville, CA: Rockridge Press.

2

Grandma's Rules to Help You Become a Cool Parent

The chapter is dedicated to the brilliant psychoanalyst Carl Jung, who reminds us that if there is anything that we wish to change in the child, we should first examine it and see whether it is not something that could better be changed in ourselves (1955). The chapter is also dedicated to Dr. Andy Burka, creative clinical psychologist and inspiring clinical supervisor who I had the great honor of working with and learning from early in my career.

In many ways, the theme and material in this chapter is a "stand alone" read. In fact, my editor and reviewers of earlier drafts suggested that I might want to expand the chapter into an entire "stand alone" trade book for parents on how to take care of yourself so that you can optimize raising kind, compassionate, caring, resilient, emotionally intelligent, well-adjusted kids. Not a bad idea! Parenting

DOI: 10.4324/9781003287070-2

is an exciting but complicated voyage full of unexpected and unanticipated challenges (Renati, Bonfiglio, & Pfeiffer, 2017). Frankly, it is daunting and a huge responsibility to raise any child in the 21st century, much less a special needs child such as a gifted student (or a child with a disability). This chapter helps parents prepare for the formidable, often unnerving, but extremely rewarding challenge.

I titled this chapter **Grandma's Rules to Help You Become a Cool Parent** because so much of what I've learned, observed, and applied in my work as a counselor, consultant, and parenting coach—as well as a parent and grandparent—has focused on teaching basic, uncomplicated, and yet important techniques, skills, and guidelines that help parents become more calm, self-assured, comfortable, and confident adults *and* parents. For simplicity's sake, I've come to call these rules and guidelines *Grandma's Rules*. One of my clients, a NASA scientist, came to call these rules, *"KISS."* Meaning "keep it simple, stupid!" Obviously, he meant that the rules weren't rocket science! In this chapter, I introduce ten. I could have called them rules, canons, or tenets; a *road map* to becoming a better-adjusted adult and more-effective parent.

Over the years, I have found these guidelines incredibly helpful in my work with adult clients. I've come to recognize that I can't coach parents to become effective and successful parents until they first learn the skills and attitudes that make them calm, reflective, compassionate, and thoughtful adults. What is nice and gratifying is that *Grandma's Rules* are supported by scientific research and considerable anecdotal clinical evidence. They are not wild-eyed personal ideas that I have "cooked-up," rules offered as a therapist "flying by the seat of my pants" in my work with parents. Not at all. These are tried-and-proven, evidence-based principles that make parenting easier and more enjoyable. And more effective!

In this chapter, I go into some detail about three of *Grandma's Rules*. At the close of the chapter, I briefly introduce an additional seven rules. I encourage the reader to spend some time delving into the resources listed at the end of the chapter. There are also excellent videos on YouTube and other social media on ways to become proficient with each of *Grandma's Rules*. The rules are easy to explain, as you will see. Yes, my NASA parent was correct—they are *KISS*. But they take an openness to self-reflection and personal change, time, commitment, and a lot of hard work, practice, and patience to master.

I suspect that you are familiar with the term "*Zen Master*." Well, in this chapter, I am talking about becoming a *Zen Master* of Grandma's Rules! Believe me, in our busy 21st century it is not easy for these tenets to become part of any adult's default approach to living each day. But once adopted, they will play a meaningful role in parenting successful, well adjusted, happy, and resilient kids! And once mastered, they do help create harmony, calmness, and authenticity in your life. *A warning: It is not easy to master these skills and attitudes—it takes practice and effort!* But it is gratifying to become proficient in Grandma's Rules. And they are effective! Okay, what follows is an introduction to *Grandma's Rules.*

Grandma's Parenting Rules

Model Good Behavior

This first core rule, tenet, or axiom is so obvious that it almost goes without saying. But it is important to remind the reader, as I always remind parents in my clinical practice, that kids—especially high ability and gifted kids—are keen observers of others' behavior. Kids' radar is set before birth to observe and pick up the many messages that they observe in their environment. It's as basic as that. My grandma preached to my brother and me, growing up in the Bronx, New York, that kids learn what they see others do, not necessarily what they are told is the right thing to do. And she was spot-on correct!

Behavioral scientists call this phenomenon *observational learning*. It is a form of social learning that starts at a very young age—among infants and toddlers! There is an abundance of research in the behavioral and neurosciences supporting observational learning. In fact, when we explore the topic of empathy and compassion later in the book, I will introduce the reader to mirror neurons as a neurophysiological basis for observational learning of empathy! Stay tuned.

Suffice to say, at this point, that kids are keen observers of important and influential adults—their parents, grandparents, and teachers, for example, and influential kids in their social world. Kids continually learn through imitating what they observe and are exposed to. What is also critically important for the reader to remember is that kids are also keen observers of undesirable and inappropriate behavior, particularly when displayed by influential adults and peers in their social world. Kids learn and imitate bad behavior just as easily as they learn good behavior through observational learning (Bandura, 1971; Frith & Frith, 2012; Pfeiffer, 2013). The gifted child who observes parents acting impulsive, punitively or uncontrollably angry, or threatening or fearfully disgusted is learning disagreeable and unattractive behavior. It's as simple as that.

On the other hand, parents who model examples of considerate and courteous behaviors, agreeable and helpful behaviors, behaviors such as gratitude—which we will discuss in subsequent chapters when I talk about *Emotional Intelligence* and *social skills*, can expect that their child will imitate these well-mannered and favorable behaviors— what social scientists call prosocial behaviors. This first tenet, **Model Good Behavior**, is such a simple, important, and powerful principle because it establishes the default interactive style of kids in their first few years of life. It is a basic and core conviction about how to interact in front of our children! Truth be told, my grandma would often say, *"Steven, you can't ever become a good parent if you continually act in immature and unacceptable ways!"* The takeaway here is never forget that kids watch and learn from how we adults act.

Change Harmful Patterns

You don't have to parent your child exactly like you were parented as a child. My grandma's second axiom was, *"Give up what your mom and dad did that wasn't so great and hold onto what they did that worked. And what made sense."* The challenge with this second tenet is that so much of how we think and behave as adults is on autopilot. I won't go as far as suggesting that all our thoughts, behaviors, and patterns of interacting are unconsciously driven. With humble respect and great veneration to Sigmund Freud and his theories on the unconscious, Freud's ideas are simply not totally correct (Mills, 2014). But research does support the notion that we typically think and behave while our brain is on autopilot. And truth be told, there are evolutionary advantages to autopilot as our default for thinking and behaving (Crane, 2009). It has kept us safe and has encouraged survival of our species!

The recent movement in positive psychology, yoga, Eastern philosophies, and in the self-help field towards *mindfulness training* is based on intentionally disengaging from automatic pilot and bringing our full awareness back to the present, to the here-and-now (Kabat-Zinn, 2018). This can be highly adaptive. And it provides us with opportunities to examine and change harmful, toxic, and destructive patterns of behavior. Patterns that compromise our ability to parent effectively. More about mindfulness shortly!

One example from my clinical practice illustrates the power of changing harmful patterns to optimize your parenting panache. A few years back, I was consulted by a bright, highly educated, and well-meaning mother who had sought out my advice because her son's preschool was alarmed with the young, gifted child's aggressive behavior with peers. My client—a successful attorney at a prestigious law firm, was raised by professional parents who, sadly, abused alcohol and characteristically interacted with one another and with their daughter—my client, with anger, irritation, rage and even fury. Apparently, these negative and destructive patterns were regularly observed, experienced, and internalized by my client— they were, regrettably, her parents' characteristic repertoire for interacting in the home. And they became almost unconsciously her own parenting style with her young preschooler.

Unbeknownst to my client, an otherwise well-educated, loving wife and caring mother, her negative and destructive pattern of parenting had become her default repertoire of interacting with her gifted, preschool son. She was not aware that she had adopted her parents' harmful parenting style. Interestingly enough, she didn't act in this characteristically toxic way with her husband. Brief counseling and mindfulness exercises[1] helped her to recognize and shed these harmful patterns, patterns that we recognize are often multi-generational. After discarding these dysfunctional patterns, she became a successful and loving parent, and champion and advocate for her young, gifted son.

This is but one example of a harmful pattern of interacting that was passed down through the generations. In my experience, over the years working with countless parents, I have heard a great many stories and observed various multigenerational dysfunctional patterns that were seemingly on autopilot. At least on autopilot until we identified and worked in counseling to change them to more functional parenting patterns. The list of harmful patterns is almost endless and I'm sure that the reader is familiar with a few from their own lived experience: parents who incessantly yell at their kids; parents who shame or threaten their kids to control them; parents who use coercive or intimidating tactics to force their kids to behave in certain ways; parents who use sarcasm and passive-aggressive comments to discipline; parents who constantly put excessive pressure on their child to succeed; parents who unduly focus on their child's grades or performance and ignore or minimize their child's effort (McCraith, 2014). These are examples of harmful patterns that are typically on autopilot. But which can be modified. Changing these dysfunctional and harmful patterns provides exciting opportunities for more kind, respectful and effective communication with your child.

Be More in the Present

"Living in the moment," is a very popular pop psychology slogan. But what exactly does this catchphrase mean? And does *being in the moment* really make a difference in the quality of one's life? And in how you parent your child? The slogan that implores us to *live in the moment*, keep our focus on the here-and-now, in fact, has a long history and a strong scientific basis. Really. The famous humanistic psychologist Abraham Maslow introduced us to his wildly popular ideas about fulfilling our innate human needs and the importance of self-actualization. Maslow contended that the ability to be in the present moment is an important component of mental wellness and self-actualization (Maslow, 1943, 1968; 1999).

Being in the present means being fully engaging with your environment, body, thinking, feelings, and emotions as they are unfolding in the moment with intention but without judgement or opinion. It is mindfulness practice incorporated into one's lifestyle. Mindfulness is an ancient concept, derived from Asian Buddhist contemplative practice, meaning "presence of mind" (Kabat-Zinn, 2018). It is not difficult to learn, and one can become proficient in a few weeks of practice. The challenge is paying close attention to the present moment—for example, becoming acutely aware of your breathing and each breath that you take. At the same time, you need to let go of all judgments (for example, no longer labeling thoughts or feelings as good or bad). In fact, breathing meditation is a common mindfulness practice.

When you are in this state of being fully in the present moment, you give your complete attention to what's happening in the here-and-now. You can see how this psychological state makes for a more engaged, attentive parent. This also isn't rocket science! Being in the moment, you no longer are the parent at your child's youth soccer game or dance practice who is repeatedly checking your iPhone for text messages, thinking about tomorrow's sales' meeting or your upcoming weekend dinner party.

Another way of thinking about mindfulness is that it is the self-regulation of our attention, while adopting an attitude of curiosity, openness to experience, and acceptance. It requires us to let go of our entrenched, automatic, and ruminative thinking. Mindfulness is a type of meditation that can be rather easily cultivated by getting in touch with the present moment. The main goal is to create greater awareness of the *"here and now"* (Niemiec, 2014).

Research shows that there are clear connections between a state of mindfulness and physical and psychological health. Practicing focused awareness and mindfulness can help reduce stress and anxiety and improve overall quality of life. There actually is neurobiological evidence for the benefits of mindfulness. Research studies applying functional magnetic resonance imaging (fMRI) technology, for example, have shown that mindfulness practice is associated with amygdala deactivation—decreasing negative emotions and enhancing emotional stability (Brown & Ryan, 2003; Lutz, Herwig, Opialla, et al., 2014).

In my own clinical practice, I have observed many concrete benefits when introducing mindfulness training to parents (and to adolescent clients!). Especially parents who report that they are in high stress jobs and find it difficult to relax or let go when they leave their work. A few examples of specific activities that can help you be more present include:

♦ **Check in with your body:** Many of my busy adult clients initially complain that they don't have ten free minutes each day to do this activity. But I insist that they build in the time. Most clients come to value this simple activity. If I were to ask you to check in with your body, I am asking you to listen to your body and be fully cognizant of every feeling, emotion, and sensation, without giving any label or meaning to what you are experiencing in the moment—well, in the ten minutes!

♦ **Schedule time to worry:** Many of my adult clients report being stressed out most of the day. This is obviously not a healthy or an adaptive, resilient way to live. It is the antithesis of a state of physical and mental health, and puts the body at risk for physiological, hormonal, and psychological crisis. The goal is to learn mindfulness and meditation to encourage a calmer, contemplative, peaceful, and lower-stress state of mind. This activity is simple: Set aside a time in your very busy days to deal with all the bothersome, high stress uncertainties that you otherwise worry about 24/7. The activity teaches you to stay calmer and more grounded in the present.

♦ **The raisin exercise:** This is a common and popular mindfulness exercise created by Kabat-Zinn (1990). It has become a standard "go-to" exercise in mindfulness training. The exercise involves taking several minutes to slowly eat one raisin while fully engaging all of one's senses. This type of Zen exercise is very powerful and tends to promote the process of savoring (Niemiec, 2014). Of course, you can substitute any number of small edibles for raisins. Try it!

◆ **Breathing exercise:** This exercise can be paired with muscle tension/relaxation or practiced as a stand-alone mediation breathing exercise. This is a popular exercise used by counselors and therapists who follow cognitive-behavioral therapy (CBT) approaches to help clients relax and better control tension, fears, and anxiety. Essentially, to practice this exercise, you need no more than three minutes and a quiet place to sit, uninterrupted. First, take a few moments to become aware of the present moment, and then concentrate and become increasingly aware of your breath. I have found that adult clients report this as one of their favorite exercises to practice at home; it is easy to build the three-minute exercise into even the busiest daily lifestyles. Kids also find this meditation exercise enjoyable and helpful. In my clinical practice, clients of all ages report that the breathing exercise increases mindfulness, helps control "mind wandering," and encourages keeping attention in the present moment.

◆ **Create a daily routine that includes time to relax:** This is another one of those simple activities that many busy and highly stressed adult clients initially find almost impossible to execute. The time to relax can be stepping away from your desk or workplace to stretch in your office chair or on the floor, do a few easy yoga exercises, go for a short walk, call a friend, take a coffee break, or listen to a favorite song or podcast. I've found this activity highly effective with even uber-busy professionals, including surgeons, physicians, trial attorneys, military, teachers, airline pilots, and police officers.

◆ **Recite a mantra:** A mantra is a word, phrase, or slogan that is recited repetitively. Originally developed in Hinduism and Buddhism, it is now widely used in the corporate world, and by high school, college, and professional athletes, and even among the elite special forces military to aid in concentration and staying in the moment. It is easy to do once you select the "right" word or phrase that holds personal meaning or power for you. It is a popular and powerful tool of meditation. For example, in my consulting with the Duke University women's soccer program, I encouraged the players to create a team slogan to help them, as a group and individually, stay focused and get through the very exhausting early morning, preseason practices. The team came up with this mantra, which worked splendidly for them: *"We got up so don't give up."* It worked for them!

Repeating a mantra or slogan in daily routines can help reduce stress and enhance calmness, buoyancy, resilience, and reinforce a positive attitude. This is an effective mindfulness activity that I routinely use with many clients. And truth be told, I use it in my personal life to remind me to stay focused and in the moment! There is no one best mantra or slogan. The beauty is taking the time to create a slogan that is personally meaningful and works for you. A few examples that some of my clients adopted for their personal use with great success: *"No pain, no gain;" "Go the extra mile;" "Hang in there;" "Go with the flow;" "I'm chasing rainbows;" "I'm cool as a cucumber;"* and *"Gotta face the music."*

◆ **Reduce your screen time:** This is a mindfulness enhancement activity that should come as no surprise to the reader. Are you aware of how much time the average adult spends viewing their iPhone, iPad, and computer screen? It may shock you. I ask my adult clients to guess, and then request that they track their screen time for one full week. Once they determine how much time, on average, they spend each day viewing social media and work-related e-mails, I challenge them to commit to reducing the time, taking social media breaks, and establishing no-phone zones in places like the bedroom, dining area, and automobile. Of course, reducing screen time provides more time to be in the moment!

◆ **Gratitude journaling:** Practicing gratitude journaling is an effective way to help adults with "wandering minds" return their focus to the present. It is a simple and yet elegant activity that involves "looking in" and self-appreciation. Taking the time each day to write down at least one aspect of your life that you are grateful for helps you control what the voices in your head tell you about yourself. It also makes you more receptive to embracing the present. I use gratitude journaling with many of my gifted clients, as well as with their parents. Gratitude journaling is part of my commitment to encourage *strengths of the heart*, which the reader will learn more about in the next chapter.

Concluding Comments

I have described three important *Grandma's Rules*. These are rules that you can easily adopt if you hope to become a better-adjusted adult and more effective parent. These are rules that I routinely introduce, discuss, teach, role play, and reinforce in my clinical work with parents. In addition to *modeling good behavior*, *changing harmful patterns*, and *being more in the present*, there are seven other *Grandma's Rules* that I routinely introduce in my work with parents. Space limitations force me to list but not detail these additional rules. They round out my "Top Ten" list:

Seven Additional Rules

- ◆ Reduce the level of stress in your life
- ◆ Learn self-compassion and self-kindness
- ◆ Learn how to keep your cool
- ◆ Try to let the little things go
- ◆ Identify and then disarm your triggers
- ◆ Create a peaceful home life
- ◆ Embrace self-care: Eat healthy, get enough sleep, exercise regularly

With practice and some guidance, you can master the above ten rules. However, they aren't easy to adopt, simply because we humans resist change. Our default mode of thinking and behaving is based on old habits and learning, automatic, autopilot, almost unconscious. At the end of the chapter, there are a list of resources that the reader can delve into to learn more about how to master *Grandma's Rules*. A key theme is that you must learn to take care of yourself as an adult if you hope to be successful parenting your gifted child (Pfeiffer, 2003; Post, 2022).

> **A disclaimer: Grandma's Rules are proven guidelines for living a healthy, satisfying life. However, they are neither intended as clinical advice nor as a substitute for direct consultation with a counselor if you are struggling with mental health concerns. It is advisable to speak with a local psychologist or counselor if you are feeling out-of-sorts, moody, unhappy, or angry. Seeking professional help for yourself or for your child is always prudent if you have specific concerns or questions that go beyond the scope of this pocketbook.**

The good news is that, in these very challenging and stressful times, you have free and readily available resources to make our parenting and marriage/partner roles easier. For example, the App Store offers, at no cost, a fairly comprehensive, science-based, and easy-to-navigate online program entitled, "In Love While Parenting." The link for the online program is: https://apps.apple.com/us/app/in-love-while-parenting/id1501984642. Enjoyable and informative online lessons include topics such as: *The long-term unhappiness chemical*; *The importance of labeling emotions*; *Sprinklers: Building deep bonds*; *Communication mistakes*; and *Recording deep bond moments* in your relationship. I have recommended to several families in my private coaching practice experimenting with this cutting-edge app; feedback has been mixed—some love it and have found it extremely informative, whereas others have found the app overly proscriptive and structured. For example, you can't move on to the next lesson until you complete all prior lessons. Bottom line: it's a cool program, and we certainly as a society are moving toward the greater use of and reliance on apps to help us navigate our lives! By the time this book is on bookstore shelves, and readily available from www.amazon.com, I am confident that there will be several other science-based, easy-to-use, and hopefully inexpensive, parenting apps. Keep your eyes open for the good ones! Also remember about the **Suggested Resources** at the end of this and every chapter.

Suggested Resources

Albers, S. (2003). *Eating mindfully*. Oakland, CA: New Harbinger Publications.

Bayda, E. (2002). *Being Zen: Bringing meditation to life*. Boston, MA: Shambhala.

Brahm, A. (2006). *Mindfulness, bliss, and beyond: A meditator's handbook*. Boston, MA: Wisdom Publications.

Clarke-Fields, H. (2019). *Raising good humans: A mindful guide to breaking the cycle of reactive parenting and raising kind, confident kids*. Oakland, CA: New Harbinger Publications.

Dalai Lama, & Cutler, H. C. (1998). *The art of happiness*. New York: Riverhead.

Goleman, D. (1997). *Healing emotions: Conversations with the Dalai Lama on mindfulness*. Boston, MA: Shambhala.

Grayson, H. (2003). *Mindful loving: 10 practices for creating deeper connections*. New York: Gotham Books.

Gunaratana, H. (2002). *Mindfulness in plain English*. Boston, MA: Wisdom Publications.

Honore, G. (2005). *In praise of slow*. London: Orion Publishing.

Kabat-Zinn, J. (2018). *Meditation is not what you think*. New York: Hyperion.

Kornfield, J., & Feldman, C. (1996). *Soul food: Stories to nourish the spirit and the heart*. New York: HarperCollins.

McCraith, S. (2014). *Yell less and love more*. Boston, MA: Four Winds Press.

Neff, K. D. (2011). *Self-compassion: Stop beating yourself up and leave insecurity behind*. New York: William Morrow.

Niemiec, R. M. (2014). *Mindfulness and character strengths: A practical guide to flourishing*. Boston, MA: Hogrefe Publishing [includes a helpful CD with mindfulness exercises].

Rivero, L. (2010). *A parent's guide to gifted teens*. Scottsdale, AZ: Great Potential Press.

Shapiro, S. & White, C. (2014). *Mindful discipline*. Oakland, CA: New Harbinger Publications.

Siegel, D. J. (2007). *The mindful brain: Reflection and attunement in the cultivation of wellbeing*. New York: Norton.

Zakoian, C. (2020). *Raising gifted children: A practical guide for parents facing big emotions and big potential.* Emeryville, CA: Rockridge Press.

Note

1 There are many self-help resources on mindfulness and meditation. The App Store offers a number of online programs, including: **Headspace: Mindful Meditation**.

References

Bandura, A. (1971). *Social learning theory*. Morristown, NJ: General Learning Press.

Brown, K. W., & Ryan, R. A. (2003). The benefits of being present: Mindfulness and its role in psychological well-being. *Journal of Personality and Social Psychology, 84* (4), 822–848.

Crane, R. (2009). *Mindfulness-based cognitive therapy*. New York: Routledge.

Frith, C. D., & Frith, U. (2012). Mechanisms of social cognition. *Annual Review of Psychology,63*, 287–313.

Jung, C. (1955). *Modern man in search of a soul*. New York: Harcourt Brace.

Kabat-Zinn, X. (1990). *Full catastrophe living using the wisdom of your body and mind to face stress, pain, and illness*. New York: Delacorte.

Kabat-Zinn, J. (2018). *Mediation is not what you think*. New York: Hyperion.

Lutz, J., Herwig, U., Opialla, S., Hittmeyer, A., Jancke, L., Rufer, M., & Bruhl, A. B. (2014). Mindfulness and emotion regulation: An fMRI study. Social Cognitive and Affective *Neuroscience, 9* (6), 776–785.

Maslow, A. (1943). A theory of human motivation. *Psychological Review, 50* (4), 370–396.

Maslow, A. (1968). *Toward a psychology of being*. New York: Van Nostrand.

Maslow, A. (1999). *Toward a psychology of being* (3rd Ed.). New York: Simon and Schuster.

McCraith, S. (2014). *Yell less love more*. Boston, MA: Fair Winds Press.

Mills, J. (2014). *Underworlds: Philosophies of the unconscious from psychoanalysis to metaphysics*. New York: Routledge.

Niemiec, R. M. (2014). *Mindfulness and character strengths*. New York: Hogrefe.

Pfeiffer, S. I. (2003). Psychological considerations in raising a healthy gifted child. In P.Olszewski-Kubilius, L. Limburg-Weber, & S. I. Pfeiffer (Eds.). *Early gifts: Recognizing and nurturing children's talents* (pp. 173–185). Waco, TX: Prufrock Press.

Pfeiffer, S. I. (2013). *Serving the gifted*. New York: Routledge.

Post, G. (2022). *The gifted parenting journey*. Goshen, KY: Gifted Unlimited.

Renati, R., Bonfiglio, N. S., & Pfeiffer, S. I. (2017). Challenges raising a gifted child: Stress and resilience factors within the family. *Gifted Education International, 33*, 145–162.

3

What Are Strengths of the Heart?

> Famous psychiatrist, author, and Holocaust survivor Viktor Frankl presciently warns us that, "For the world is in a bad state, but everything will become still worse unless each of us does his best" (1959).

I am pleased that you completed the chapter on **Grandma's Rules** and are now ready to focus on *strengths of the heart*! I hope that you found the preceding chapter informative. And relevant to your own personal life. The material in the previous chapter provides a foundational summary of my work with parents in encouraging social intelligence, "soft skills." What I call, *strengths of the heart*. As you by now recognize, I emphasize the importance of "taking care of yourself" if you hope to do right for your kids. To be a model that you want your kids to emulate, you must have your own life in order! Here's one example from my consulting practice. I was working with a parent who was overly pessimistic and even cynical about most things in her life. She was an anxious, angry, and fearful parent. This toxicity derailed her otherwise sincere attempts to

DOI: 10.4324/9781003287070-3

effectively parent. In counseling, we worked to first change her negative view of the world so that it didn't inadvertently spill over to parenting her daughter. Okay, with that introduction, let's talk about what *strengths of the heart* are and why they are important.

In the first chapter, I hinted that my early thinking on *strengths of the heart* originated from work in my research lab while at Florida State University, and before that, at Duke University. My early ideas on *strengths of the heart* were also formulated from observations of the clients that I worked with in my clinical practice, and in conversations with a great many parents at workshops that I have led. I was determined to better understand the social and emotional lives of gifted kids and young adults (for example, see Neihart, Pfeiffer, & Cross, 2015). And I was resolute in understanding why many bright kids don't grow up to be successful, resilient, well-adjusted, and happy adults.

My early work also focused on what parents might be able to do to nudge, encourage, and guide their gifted child onto a success trajectory (Pfeiffer, 2013a, 2017). This steered our research lab to examine the emerging literature on strength-based interventions and explore the exciting work in positive psychology. I was determined to understand how, as an academic clinician, I could support gifted kids and their parents who might be at risk for social-emotional, behavioral, or psychological problems. And as executive director of a large, summer residential gifted program on the campus of Duke University, I was committed to encouraging the well-being and health promotion of the more than one thousand gifted kids under my watch.

Based as much on my clinical experience and conversations with a great many parents of gifted kids as on published research, I came to understand that most gifted kids who are successful in life possess three important characteristics or traits. Back in 1998, I originally named these three traits, *"strengths of the heart and soul."* I later nicknamed them *"soft heart skills"* at parent talks and workshops. The nickname morphed over time to the more popular term, *strengths of the heart*. The three traits that make up "heart strengths"—called by other researchers as "soft skills" or "SEL skills"—represent important social-emotional skills. These soft skills make a real difference in the lives of all kids, not only gifted kids (Greenberg, et al., 2003; Jones, Greenberg, & Crowley, 2015; Suldo, Hearon, & Shaunessy-Dedrick, 2018).

The three traits that, together, make up *strengths of the heart* are *Emotional Intelligence*, *character strengths*, and *social skills*. Collectively, when these three traits are fully operative, considerable research and an abundance of anecdotal evidence suggests that they make a huge difference in successful life outcomes. Life outcomes for gifted kids such as resilience, robust mental health, happiness, job success, and subjective well-being (Kennedy-Moore, 2019; Niemiec, 2018; Pfeiffer, 2013a, 2017).

Emotional Intelligence was the first of the three *super traits* that we investigated in the search for why not all gifted kids grow up to be well-adjusted, successful, and resilient young adults. Most clinicians, researchers, and popular writers view Emotional Intelligence as the ability to understand, read, and control one's own and others' emotions. Many scientists and practitioners recognize that Emotional Intelligence consists of important cognitive and social-interpersonal skills necessary to be successful in life. More will be presented on Emotional Intelligence in Chapter 4—so, please be patient!

In my early work as executive director of the Duke University gifted program—as far back as 1998, my writings suggested that high Emotional Intelligence might perhaps be the singular, *magic bullet* that protects all kids, including gifted kids, from experiencing the negative effects of trauma, psychological suffering, and social-emotional distress (Pfeiffer, 2001). At the time, I wasn't considering the other two traits—character strengths and social skills—in my pursuit of a *Holy Grail* for optimal mental health. Quite frankly, I was hedging my bets on the power of Emotional Intelligence, alone. Parenthetically, I had met Daniel Goleman, popular, bestselling science writer who many consider the father of Emotional Intelligence—at a conference and was taken by his compelling personal stories about the power of Emotional Intelligence. After meeting him, I was captivated and hooked.

However, I came to recognize my gaffe in thinking that Emotional Intelligence was the panacea or tonic for the many social, familial, and emotional stressors that gifted kids might encounter. My research teams at Duke, and later at Florida State University, conducted applied research and developed a pilot measure of Emotional Intelligence to test the purported power of Emotional Intelligence. At the time, we were fervent believers in the potential power of Emotional Intelligence!

However, painstaking, hard-nosed, and honest analysis of our work proved disappointing. Our research indicated that **Emotional Intelligence**, although a provocative, appealing, and potentially important psychological construct, in its own right (Zeidner & Matthews, 2017), was *not* the stand-alone, prophylactic cure-all that guarantees resilience, well-being, and successful life outcomes (Pfeiffer, 2013a, 2018). We concluded that Emotional

Intelligence played a modest, "statistically significant" but not large role in explaining important life outcomes such as vibrant mental health, well-being, friendships, happiness, and resilience.

Okay, so we were left with the disappointing conclusion that Emotional Intelligence wasn't the decisive, single cure-all trait for the many challenges that befall kids. We began a search for a better answer. We asked, *"what might explain why some, but not all, gifted kids are successful, well-adjusted, and resilient in adult life?"* We scoured the published literature in search of any factors, skills or traits that help explain what keeps gifted kids within the *guard rails*, on a path toward resilience, happiness, optimism, well-being, and life success.

Our search also relied on my first-hand experience as executive director of the Duke gifted summer program and co-director of the Florida Governor's School for Science and Space Technology. I spent long hours thinking about the many well-adjusted bright and talented kids that I had the pleasure of working with and getting to know personally on the campuses of Duke University and Kennedy Space Center, site of the pilot Florida Governor's School. One quiet afternoon, enjoying a cup of coffee, I had an epiphany. I still considered Emotional Intelligence important. But it hit me, almost like a lightning bolt, that many of the well-adjusted, highly motivated, joyful, contented, and goal-directed gifted kids on the campuses of Duke University and Kennedy Space Center seemed to have well-developed **social skills**. Social skills such as a comfort with taking turns, listening respectfully and not interrupting peers or counselors, being polite, considerate, helpful, kind, displaying good manners, getting along well with others—both peers and adults, easily developing friendships, and generally being well-liked. I had found my second *magic bullet*—social skills!

Conversations with hundreds of parents, educators, and mental health practitioners confirmed that kids who lacked or didn't display age-expected or culturally normative social skills were more likely to be unhappy, without friends, and oftentimes despondent, emotionally detached, and troubled (Kennedy-Moore, 2019; Pfeiffer & Prado, 2022; Seligman, Steen, Park, & Peterson, 2005). Our own research and tons of comments at parent workshops corroborated what was described in published studies— social skills are immensely helpful for building resiliency and well-being in gifted kids (Pfeiffer, 2018; Pfeiffer et al., 2016; Proyer, Gander, & Tandler, 2017). We found our second *super trait*. A second guard-rail that keeps gifted kids on a success path!

Not long after, I came upon the third and final *super trait* for my strengths of the heart model. Our research team was still searching for any possible traits that we might have missed. We wanted to be certain that we established a complete picture of what would assure that gifted kids would grow up to be well-adjusted, cheerful, successful, and resilient young adults. The final puzzle piece proved to be **character strengths**! Considerable research supported this idea (Seligman, Steen, Park, & Peterson, 2005). For example, a large-scale study that looked at kindergarten social competence and future adult wellness confirmed that character strengths such as empathy, compassion, and kindness made a huge difference in favorable life outcomes (Jones, Greenberg, & Crowley, 2015).

Our own research investigated the group of character strengths first presented by Peterson and Seligman (2004). We explored tests that measure character strengths to identify which scales and even test items might make a real difference in the lives of bright kids. We collected and cataloged measures of empathy, kindness, forgiveness, openness to experience, honesty, humility, optimism, gratitude, courage, and compassion. Our lab investigated the character strength taxonomy proposed by Peterson and Seligman, seeking those strengths easiest to measure and most relevant in the lives lived by successful gifted kids (Pfeiffer, 2018). More on this exciting work in Chapter 5. I don't want to steal too much of the thunder about character strengths and *signature strengths of the heart* at this moment. Suffice to say, for a great many gifted kids, character strengths such as humility, gratitude, open-mindedness, honesty, and kindness make a huge difference in building resilience and leading to favorable life outcomes (Pfeiffer, 2017).

Concluding Comments

Remember in the very first chapter the story about Claudio, the troubled residential student attending the Duke gifted summer program. Claudio was brought to my office because he was ensnared in a heated and unpleasant argument with his teacher and a few of his fellow classmates. His instructor brought Claudio to me because he was acting in a disrespectful and challenging way. Claudio was unwilling to politely accept the differing opinions and views of his fellow classmates—a sign of a deficit in age-appropriate social skills. I also wondered if Claudio's ill-mannered behavior might be because of a low level of empathy and an inability to understand other classmates' thinking—a problem with what we psychologists call *theory of mind*. Theory of mind refers to a person's ability to understand other people by ascribing independent mental states to them. It requires a person to understand that another person's thinking may be different from their own. That other persons might hold different values, beliefs, desires, intentions, emotions, and ideas. A functional theory of mind is essential for success in everyday social interactions. Gifted kids "on the autism spectrum," for example—what we call twice exceptional gifted kids with Asperger's syndrome, are often challenged because they lack a theory of mind.

Claudio sat across from me with an angry, brooding scowl. He was in no mood to recognize, much less discuss, what had triggered his boorish and frightful mood. It didn't take a Scotland Yard detective to see that he was not going to talk with me about why he was unable to keep his cool during a heated classroom discussion. This incident—early in my tenure at Duke, of a highly intellectually gifted young man acting rather dumb—totally losing his cool and melting down to the point where he was unable to manage his emotions under the pressure of a spirited classroom discussion—became a watershed moment in my work with the gifted. It was an epiphany for me. It set the stage for my beginning to think about *strengths of the heart*. It actually encouraged me, twenty years later, to develop a parent rating scale that measures *strengths of the heart*, the *Gifted Rating Scales*™ 2 (Pfeiffer & Jarosewich, 2023).

The incident with Claudio helped me understand that many fabulously bright students—intellectually gifted kids—with magnificent *head strengths*, don't always have nearly as well-developed soft skills or *heart strengths*. Claudio didn't have a psychiatric disorder. That was not the reason for his challenging classroom behavior. Claudio didn't even have what we clinicians call a *subclinical* psychiatric degree of distress (Pfeiffer, 2013b; Post, 2022). His problem was that he lacked important, age-appropriate social skills, a healthy dosage of Emotional Intelligence, and strong character strength—*strengths of the heart*. In my experience, many gifted kids with social skill deficits, low levels of Emotional Intelligence, and undeveloped character strength are misdiagnosed in the schools as having a psychiatric disorder such as ADHD or Asperger's.

As I've described in this chapter, what I mean by heart strengths—as distinguished from head strengths—are those important soft skills and personal assets in the areas of social maturity, ability to understand, read, and control one's own and others' emotions, communicate effectively with others, utilize age-appropriate and culturally sensitive social skills, and be kind, empathic, humble, compassionate, tactful, and agreeable. These are what I have come to call *strengths of the heart*. They make a real difference in the lives of gifted kids. More about them in the following chapters. What follows are a list of suggested resources for those interested in digging deeper into the topics covered in this chapter.

Suggested Resources

Brooks. D. (2016). *The road to character*. New York: Random House.

Carter, S. L. (1996). *Integrity*. New York: Basic Books.

Delisle, J. R. (2018). *Understanding your gifted child from the inside out: A guide to the social and emotional lives of gifted kids*. New York: Routledge.

Kennedy-Moore, E. (2019). *Kid confidence: Help your child make friends, build resilience, and develop real self-esteem.* Oakland, CA: New Harbinger Publications.

Lewis, B. A. (2005). *What do you stand for? For teens: A guide to building character.* Minneapolis, MN: Free Spirit Publishing.

Owen, D. (2023). New book series "Better Than Therapy": *Everyone feels angry sometimes; Everyone feels anxious sometimes; Everyone feels sad sometimes.* www.puppydogsandicecream.com

Pfeiffer, S. I. (2013b). *Serving the gifted.* New York: Routledge.

Reuben, S. C. (1997). *Children of character: A parent's guide.* Santa Monica, CA: Canter & Associates.

References

Greenberg, M. T., Weissberg, R. P., O'Brien, M. U., et al. (2003). Enhancing school-based prevention and youth development through coordinated social, emotional, and academic learning. *American Psychologist, 58* (6/7), 466–474.

Jones, D. E., Greenberg, M., & Crowley, M. (2015). Early social-emotional functioning and public health: The relationship between kindergarten social competence and future wellness. *American Journal of Public Health, 195,* 2283–2290.

Kennedy-Moore, E. (2019). Kid confidence: *Help your child make friends, build resilience, and develop self-esteem.* Oakland, CA: New Harbinger Publications.

Neihart, M., Pfeiffer, S. I., & Cross, T. (Eds.) (2015). *The social and emotional development of gifted children: What we know* (2nd Ed.). Waco, TX: Prufrock Press.

Niemiec, R. M. (2018). *Character strengths interventions.* New York: Hogrefe.

Peterson, C., & Seligman, M. E. P. (2004). *Character strengths and virtues: A handbook and classification.* Oxford: Oxford University Press.

Pfeiffer, S. I. (2001). Emotional intelligence: Popular but elusive construct. *Roeper Review, 23*, 138–142.

Pfeiffer, S. I. (2013a). Lessons learned from working with high-ability students. *Gifted Education International, 29*, 86–97.

Pfeiffer, S. I. (2013b). *Serving the gifted.* New York: Routledge.

Pfeiffer, S. I. (2017). Success in the classroom and in life: Focusing on strengths of the head and strengths of the heart. *Gifted Education International, 33*, 95–101.

Pfeiffer, S. (2018). Understanding success and psychological well-being: Focusing on strengths of the heart. *Brazilian Journal of Psychological Studies, 35*, 259–263.

Pfeiffer, S. I., & Jarosewich, T. (2023). *Gifted Rating Scales™ 2.* Toronto: MHS Assessments.

Pfeiffer, S. I., & Prado, R. M. (2022). Strengths of the heart and social-emotional learning: Present status and future opportunities. In A. Rocha, R. G. Perales, A. Ziegler, J. S. Perales, J. S. Renzulli, F. Gagné, S. I. Pfeiffer, & T. Lubart (Eds.), *Educational inclusion in high capacities: Arguments and perspectives. Arguments and perspectives* (pp. 245–269). Porto: ANÉIS.

Pfeiffer, S. I., Valler, E. C., Burko, J. A., Yarnell, J. B., Branagan, A. M., Smith, S. M., Barbash, E., & Saintil, M. (2016). Focusing on strengths of the heart in understanding success and psychological well-being of high-ability students. *Austin Child and Adolescent Psychiatry, 1*, 1002.

Post, G. (2022). *The gifted parenting journey.* Goshen, KY: Gifted Unlimited.

Proyer, R. T., Gander, F., & Tandler, N. (2017). Strength-based interventions: Their importance in application to the gifted. *Gifted Education International, 33*, 118–130.

Seligman, M. E. P., Steen, T. A., Park, N., & Peterson, C. (2005). Positive psychology progress: Empirical validation of interventions, *American Psychologist, 60*, 410–421.

Suldo, S. M., Hearon, B. V., & Shaughness-Dedrick, E. (2018). Examining gifted students' mental health through the lens of positive psychology. In S. I. Pfeiffer (Ed.). *APA handbook of giftedness and talent* (pp. 433–449). Washington, DC: American Psychological Association Books.

Zeidner, M., & Matthews, G. (2017). Emotional intelligence in gifted students. *Gifted Education International, 33*, 163–182.

4

Emotional Intelligence Makes a Difference

Special call-out and appreciation to author Michele Borba, who warns us that "running on empty [is] raising a generation of strivers, not thrivers" (2021).

What Is EI?

The reader is probably wondering, *what exactly does it mean to be emotionally intelligent. Does it really matter? Is Emotional Intelligence something that can be learned? Does Emotional Intelligence make a difference in my kid's life?* As you know, being book smart doesn't guarantee success or happiness in life. Book smarts doesn't assure that your bright child will be resilient and well adjusted. We all agree that high IQ is nice to be blessed with and a good predictor of life success. Don't let anyone try to convince you otherwise! But high IQ falls short of guaranteeing your gifted child

DOI: 10.4324/9781003287070-4

a successful life (Pfeiffer, 2013, 2015). Street smarts is also important! Street smarts is, in fact, really a slang or colloquial way of describing what we psychologists mean by people who are experts at making finer-grained distinctions when perceiving, understanding, predicting, and categorizing emotions. The fancy term is *"emotional granularity."* It is also called Emotional Intelligence!

As I already mentioned, author Daniel Goleman (1995) sparked my early interest and preliminary thinking about Emotional Intelligence. In his best-selling book, and in his popular live talks and podcasts, Goleman proposes that Emotional Intelligence consists of a large constellation of blended competencies and dispositions, such as self-awareness, self-regulation of behavior, social skills, empathy, and even motivation—in many ways, what I've described as social intelligence, soft skills, and ultimately, *strengths of the heart* (Pfeiffer, 2003; Pfeiffer & Prado, 2022; Pfeiffer et al. 2016). Many ultimately criticized Goleman's views on Emotional Intelligence as fuzzy and too all-encompassing, myself included (Pfeiffer, 2001).

The first scientific paper describing a theory of Emotional Intelligence was published in 1990, appearing in the journal *Imagination, Cognition, and Personality.* The authors were John Mayer and Peter Salovey (Mayer, Salovey, & Caruso, 2000, 2002).

These two groundbreaking scientists, Mayer and Salovey, proposed that emotions are important sources of information, and that Emotional Intelligence helps us understand and solve problems and guide our social interactions. Their elegant theory essentially suggested that if you are the kind of person who can accurately read your own emotions and put your feelings into words, skillful at reading the emotions of others, and adept in managing your own emotions, then you are emotionally intelligent. They developed the very first measure of Emotional Intelligence, called the *MSCEIT*—which our research lab used in several of our own studies (Pfeiffer & Muniz Prado, 2022; Pfeiffer & Valler, 2016). The *MSCEIT* test of Emotional Intelligence looks at how well a person perceives emotions, uses emotions, understands emotions, and manages emotions. Coincidentally, the *MSCEIT* is published by the same test publisher, Multi-Health Systems (MHS), which publishes the *GRS*™ 2, the rating scale that I developed to measure strengths of the heart (Pfeiffer & Jarosewich, 2023).

Mayer and Salovey were also among the first researchers to confirm that high scores on their *MSCEIT* scale and other measures of Emotional Intelligence were related to important life outcomes. Our own measure, the *GRS*™ 2, confirms Mayer and Salovey's findings. Mayer and Salovey broke important ground in demonstrating that kids and adults can learn the skills underlying Emotional Intelligence. This was a hugely important finding. It affords you as a parent (and teachers) the opportunity to teach your child to become savvier in the Emotional Intelligence skills essential to street smarts.

Recently, Professor Lisa Feldman Barrett, expert on the neurobiology and social psychology of emotions, challenged the time-honored, "classical" view of emotions—that we all have the same emotions, built-in from birth. Her groundbreaking book, *How Emotions Are Made*, draws on contemporary research to challenge the classical view that our emotions are artifacts of evolution, instinctual reflexes at odds with rational thinking. This classical view dates to Plato, Hippocrates, Aristotle, the Buddha, Freud, and Darwin. Feldman Barrett offers a radically different and compelling view: emotions are constructed, not an inherent part of our animal nature. For each of us, emotions are our brain's unique creation—how we each interpret our bodily sensations (Feldman Barrett, 2017). Feldman Barrett argues that our brain, consisting of 86 billion neurons—connected into vast networks, continually creates, and revises our mental model of the world. Her brilliant and original ideas on the science of emotions have profound implications for how we view Emotional Intelligence. And her ideas speak to why it is beneficial to help your child learn to make finer-grained distinctions about their emotional experiences. To become *emotional experts*. Much of my thinking about the practical implications of how to help gifted kids become emotional experts ("emotional granularity") is based on the singularly novel ideas proposed by Feldman Barrett.

Why EI Matters

It is probably most easy to make a case for the value and importance of Emotional Intelligence by describing what it looks like. People high in Emotional Intelligence tend to have superior mental health, greater school and employment success, and strong leadership skills. As I mentioned above, people high in Emotional Intelligence are better able to discriminate between different emotions and label them more precisely and appropriately. People with high Emotional Intelligence are superior in the use of emotional information to guide their thinking and behavior. And they are better able to keep cool under pressure, motivate themselves to get things done, influence other people, and remain positive during difficult situations. Sounds like what you'd want your gifted child to be savvy at, right?

People high in Emotional Intelligence tend to avoid excessively focusing on bad feelings and consciously try not to wallow in bad feelings. Because they can better understand how others feel—a type of empathy and perspective taking, they have a huge advantage in managing social situations that otherwise create huge difficulties for many gifted kids. Recall the example of Claudio, the bright Duke student who lacked social intelligence and street smarts—and control of his negative emotions. This contributed to his misreading emotional signals and, as a result, antagonizing and aggravating his peers and instructors!

Kids high in Emotional Intelligence are better at managing stress, building positive relationships with other peers, dealing more calmly with teachers and parents, and being a team player. Emotionally intelligent kids look after their own needs, but they also consider the needs of others. They are thoughtful and solicitous. They aren't self-centered or egotistical. Finally, and particularly relevant to my argument, gifted kids high in Emotional Intelligence are more prone to display advanced social skills and better developed character strengths. Emotional Intelligence tends to go hand-in-glove with advanced social skills and better developed character assets—the triple package of strengths of the heart! There is a powerful synergy among the three heart strengths!

Most of the theorizing and research about Emotional Intelligence has focused on adults, not kids. Psychologists and organizational consultants have used EQ tests in the corporate world to measure Emotional Intelligence and encourage employees to grow their EQ or emotional quotient. The most popular adult EQ test is the *EQ-i*, a self-report measure of Emotional Intelligence developed by Israeli Professor Reuven Bar-On (Bar-On, 2002). The *EQ-i* has been translated into over 30 languages (Stein, 2009). The *EQ-i* measures five areas of emotional and social intelligence: intra-personal competencies or know yourself abilities, interpersonal or "people skills;" adaptability, flexibility and problem-solving; stress management; and general mood. Items on the *EQ-i* assess sensitivity to the feelings of others, kindness toward others, optimistic attitude, level of self-control, and perceived friendliness. Mayer, Salovey, Reuven Bar-On, and I all believe that people can learn to raise their EQ (Pfeiffer, 2015), as I will explain.

General Tips on Promoting Emotional Intelligence

Helping your gifted child become more "emotionally granular" provides them with social-emotional tools to make finer distinctions among their feelings. Remember Lisa Feldman Barrett's theory of constructed emotions—that our brain constructs everything we experience, including emotions. Emotions are made, not passively triggered. In her theory, your child is the architect of their thinking and their emotions. With your guidance, your child can learn to make finer-grained emotional distinctions on the road to becoming emotional experts!

For example, many kids use only a limited vocabulary of words to describe all their pleasant and unpleasant feelings—using the word "awesome" when they experience anything pleasant and "crummy" when they experience anything unpleasant. This limits a more extensive, refined, and subtle language of affect and feelings. As a parent, you can teach your child to expand their language of feelings. One easy way to help your kid expand their vocabulary of emotions is to discuss examples of emotional expression from your everyday experience, from characters in storybooks, from actors that your kids are familiar with on TV shows, watching YouTube vignettes and even cartoon characters in movies. There are literally tons of instances occurring in the media, at school, in home and in the neighborhood, on film and in books, which provide excellent opportunities for you to converse about the myriad of feelings that your child might be experiencing. These are what we psychologists call teachable moments to expand your child's emotion concepts!

Help your gifted kid learn new feeling words. The more fine-grained their vocabulary, the more precisely their brain can calibrate what they are experiencing. And they can also learn which feeling words to use and when. This is analogous to the developed skill of painters learning to see fine distinctions in color, tone, hue, and shading. Even with very young kids, you can teach feeling words as a fun activity to expand their Emotional Intelligence. You can have your child act out the words, role play the feeling words, draw pictures of figures expressing the feeling words.

As your child's parent, you can regularly talk about what causes emotions and what are the consequences to others. You can certainly demonstrate by sharing personal experiences. Parents of older gifted kids, for example, can talk about when they have experienced the negative feelings of shame and guilt, helping your older gifted child learn the subtle distinction between the two. Guilt comes from thinking that we did a bad thing. And shame arises from the more global judgment that we are a bad person. Parents can talk about how they managed when they felt guilt or shame. No parent is perfect. Don't be afraid to tell your gifted child about exactly how and when you've handled these emotional situations well, and when you blew it.

Provide instances from your own world when you've reacted with impatience, frustration, disappointment, exasperation, resentment, annoyance, boredom, antagonism, confusion, pride, curiosity embarrassment, relief, envy, surprise, even anger. Kids love to hear about how the important adults in their lives react to unpleasant feelings that challenge our ability to stay cool and calm. Don't be reluctant to talk about the bad and ugly, as well as the good ways that you handled your emotions! Telling empowering stories about how you struggled and triumphed can teach important lessons about Emotional Intelligence (Kennedy-Moore, 2019).

What else can you do to promote Emotional Intelligence? You can ask open-ended questions, just like we therapists do in counseling! For example, it is better to ask your gifted child, *"Tell me how you are feeling now?"* rather than a more closed question like, *"Are you upset?"* You can also be a powerful role model for your child by discussing their own feelings and emotions. And sharing how they have learned to master their emotions. Remember when I spoke about *Grandma's Rule* of the influence and sway that you have when you model the kinds of behavior, attitudes, and values that you want your child to adopt and embrace.

For example, if your gifted child is feeling anxious before a big test or upcoming school play, you could talk about how you have learned to master similarly unpleasant feelings. Counselors teach the Buddhist technique of recategorization of emotions as one useful strategy in these kinds of situations. You advise your child to interpret the queasy and unpleasant feelings in their stomach not as fear or anxiety, but rather as *"the body getting ready to be courageous,"* or *"grit."* The message and *"gift"* that you are communicating to your child is that, yes, you have unpleasant feelings in your stomach, but you can relabel these unpleasant sensations as your body's signal to be courageous and brave.

You can encourage your children to use *journaling* to reflect on how they felt during the day, writing down both negative and positive interactions. You can teach your children the skills involved in *active listening*. For example, helping your child to paraphrase what they hear and use nonverbal cues like nodding. You can use *puppets* with younger gifted kids to teach feelings. Puppets are excellent tools to help young kids act out different social situations. For example, have one puppet take a toy from another puppet and ask your child what emotion or emotions the puppet might be feeling. After your child labels the emotion, you can then encourage them to talk about what it feels like when a friend or classmate doesn't share. Finally, there are many excellent video training programs on the Internet about emotions and feelings. In researching online resources for this chapter, I found over a dozen excellent YouTube videos depicting 7 to 21 different facial expression emotions, based on the illuminating and influential work of Professor Paul Ekman (2003) on facial expressions. This is fun stuff to view with your child to help them become savvier in recognizing different facial expressions.

Family meetings are an excellent way to teach kids the many skills underlying Emotional Intelligence. I discuss how to run *family meetings* in the next chapter. I am a strong advocate that parents schedule weekly family meetings. Family meetings provide a unique, nonjudgmental venue that supports an open and nonthreatening dialogue among family members. Family meetings are a wonderful opportunity for parents to talk about Emotional Intelligence. And to talk about character strengths and social skills. Essentially, *family meetings* are designed to resolve family disagreements and conflicts, clarify rules and roles, and promote family harmony, respect, improved communication, intimacy, and new social-emotional skills (Pfeiffer, 2003).

Concluding Comments

Street smart kids, those adept at the skills underlying Emotional Intelligence, are better able to discriminate between different emotions and more adept at labeling feelings precisely and appropriately. Kids higher in Emotional Intelligence, especially when they also have well-developed social skills and character strengths, are better able to keep cool under pressure, motivate themselves to get things done, influence other people, and remain positive during difficult situations. They avoid excessively focusing on bad feelings. Because they can better understand how others feel, they have a huge advantage in managing social situations that otherwise create huge difficulties for many gifted kids.

Helping your gifted child to become savvier in the skills underlying Emotional Intelligence provides them with a huge advantage. As you will read in the next two chapters, when combined with savvy social skills and well-developed character strengths, you are giving your child the vital, synergistic gift of social-emotional skills to live a successful, meaningful, resilient, and successful life. Below are some suggested resources for those readers interested in delving deeper into Emotional Intelligence.

Suggested Resources

Ekman, P. (2003). *Emotions revealed*. New York: Times Books.
Feldman Barrett, L. (2017). *How emotions are made: The secret life of the brain*. Boston, MA: Mariner.
Goleman, D. (1995). *Emotional intelligence: Why it can matter more than IQ*. New York: Bantam.
Gottman, J. (1998). *Raising an emotionally intelligent child*. New York: Simon & Schuster.
Perez, K. (2021). *The social-emotional toolbox*. Baltimore, MD: Brookes.
Stein, S. J. (2009). *Emotional intelligence for dummies*. New York: Wiley.
Zaki, J. (2019). *The war for kindness: Building empathy in a fractured world*. New York: Crown.

References

Bar-On, R. (2002). *Bar-On Emotional Quotient Inventory: Short Form (EQi;S): Technical manual*. Toronto: Multi-Health Systems.
Borba, M. (2021). *Thrivers: The surprising reasons why some kids struggle and others shine*. New York: Putnam.
Ekman, P. (2003). *Emotions revealed*. New York: Times Books.
Feldman Barrett, L. (2017). *How emotions are made: The secret life of the brain*. Boston, MA: Mariner.
Goleman, D. (1995). *Emotional intelligence: Why it can matter more than IQ*. New York: Bantam Books.
Kennedy-Moore, E. (2019). *Kid confidence: Help your child make friends, build resilience, and develop self-esteem*. Oakland, CA: New Harbinger Publications.

Mayer, J. D., & Salovey, P., & Caruso, D. (2000). Models of Emotional Intelligence. In R. J. Sternberg (Ed.), *Handbook of intelligence* (pp. 396–420). New York: Cambridge University Press.

Mayer, J. D., & Salovey, P., & Caruso, D. (2002). *The MSCEIT—User's manual*. Toronto: Multi-Health Systems.

Pfeiffer, S. I. (2001). Emotional intelligence: Popular but elusive construct. *Roeper Review, 23*, 138–142.

Pfeiffer, S. I. (2003). Psychological considerations in raising a healthy gifted child. In P. Olszewski-Kubilius, L. Limburg-Weber, & S. I. Pfeiffer (Eds.). *Early gifts: Recognizing and nurturing children's talents* (pp. 173–185). Waco, TX: Prufrock Press.

Pfeiffer, S. I. (2013). *Serving the gifted*. New York: Routledge.

Pfeiffer, S. I. (2015). *Essentials of gifted assessment*. Hoboken, NJ: Wiley.

Pfeiffer, S. I., & Jarosewich, T. (2023). *Gifted Rating Scales™ 2*. Toronto: MHS Assessments.

Pfeiffer, S. I., & Prado, R. M. (2022). Strengths of the heart and social-emotional learning: Present status and future opportunities. In A. Rocha, R. G. Perales, A. Ziegler, J. S. Perales, J. S. Renzulli, F. Gagné, S. I. Pfeiffer, & T. Lubart (Eds.), *Educational inclusion in high capacities: Arguments and perspectives. Arguments and perspectives* (pp. 245–269). Porto: ANÉIS.

Pfeiffer, S. I., Valler, E. C., Burko, J. A., Yarnell, J. B., Branagan, A. M., Smith, S. M., Barbash, E., & Saintil, M. (2016). Focusing on strengths of the heart in understanding success and psychological well-being of high-ability students. *Austin Child and Adolescent Psychiatry, 1*, 1002.

Stein, S. J. (2009). *Emotional intelligence for dummies*. New York: Wiley.

5

Character Strengths Make a Difference

Henry David Thoreau purportedly once said, "Could a greater miracle take place than for us to look through each other's eyes for an instant?" And Stephen Covey, popular author of, *The 7 Habits of Highly Effective People* writes, "Most of us spend too much time on what is urgent and not enough time on what is important."

What Are Character Strengths?

Early in my tenure as headmaster of the Duke University gifted summer program, I recognized that high IQ alone did not shield bright kids from social, behavioral, and emotional difficulties. As you have already read, I came to realize that Emotional Intelligence and age-appropriate social skills were both important in the lives of resilient, successful, vibrant gifted kids. I came to appreciate that a third super trait played an important role in terms of

DOI: 10.4324/9781003287070-5

which gifted kids were successful and resilient—character strengths. Character strengths proved to be the final missing puzzle piece in my triple package strengths of the heart! Kids on the Duke campus who had self-awareness, were able to regulate their emotions and take the perspective of others, had solid, age-appropriate social skills, and possessed empathy, kindness, humility, optimism, gratitude, and compassion tended to make friends easier, get along better with peers and instructors, and were spirited and resilient in the face of challenges and adversity. They also avoided interpersonal troubles and difficulties. In character strengths we found the final puzzle piece to the total elixir, a triple package of people skills that makes a real difference in bright kids' lives.

Why Character Strengths Matter?

Remember that Emotional Intelligence is the ability to understand and control one's own emotions and to accurately read how other people are feeling. And recall that social skills are the way that kids effectively and smoothly communicate socially and interpersonally. Examples of social skills include taking turns without complaining, listening before speaking, not interrupting peers, being polite, considerate, and helpful, and having good manners. Emotional Intelligence and social skills matter in the lives of gifted kids. So do character strengths! Considerable research indicates that character strengths facilitate kids' ability to establish and maintain healthy and rewarding relationships. Character strengths help kids make constructive and smart decisions and avoid unduly risky choices. Character strengths lead to more successful life outcomes and more buoyant well-being for your child (Jones et al., 2015; Peterson & Seligman, 2004; Pfeiffer, 2017; Weissberg et al., 2015).

At my lab at Duke University and later, at Florida State University, my students and I researched the character strengths first identified by Peterson and Seligman (2004). Peterson and Seligman created an ingenious taxonomy of 24-character strengths and virtues. In our lab, we began collecting and cataloguing measures of empathy, kindness, forgiveness, openness to experience, humility, self-reflection, courage, optimism, gratitude, and compassion. We developed our own measure of character strengths, which was a prototype and the forerunner of my *Gifted Rating Scales™ 2*, published by MHS this year. Our lab conducted dozens of research studies to determine which character strengths might be particularly important in the lives of gifted kids. We hoped to identify a possible subset of *signature character strengths* that made a real difference in promoting resilience and well-being. Our research complemented the work of Darling-Hammond (2015), Durlak, Domitrovich, Weisberg, and Gullotta (2015), and Suldo, Hearon, and Shaunessy-Dedrick et al. (2018).

I won't take up too much space discussing our research. Admittedly, it is a bit dry! But our research did confirm our initial hunch that character strengths matter. For example, we ran focus groups of teachers to test the perceived importance of various character strengths. Our lab invited parents to complete measures of Emotional Intelligence, character strengths, life satisfaction, emotionality, problem-solving, stress and coping—and examined the inter-relationships among the large datasets. Character strength items representing humility, optimism, gratitude, kindness, passion, persistence, love of learning, honesty, and compassion correlated significantly with positive life outcomes. And correlated significantly with social skills and Emotional Intelligence (Pfeiffer & Blankenship, 2017).

In another set of studies, we invited groups of parents, teachers, and gifted kids to rank order a large list of adjectives. Some of the adjectives represented "head strengths," words like *creative, witty, bright, logical, industrious,* and *original.* Other adjectives denoted "heart strengths," words like *loving, patient, tolerant,* and *understanding.* We included filler words, such as outgoing, independent, versatile, dominant, and spunky. We asked the parents, teachers, and kids to rank order the most important qualities that people could possess. Across hundreds of different raters—kids, teachers, and parents, the ten highest rated adjectives were *all* character strengths. All ten! The top ten-rated adjectives were: *good-hearted, caring, friendly, kind, helpful, sensitive, compassionate, sociable, likeable,* and *honest.* Our data confirmed what the Greek philosopher Plato said over 2,400 years ago about living a harmonious life of virtue!

Truth be told, our research did *not* identify a smaller subset of preeminent character strengths. For some gifted kids, playfulness, gratitude, love of learning, and social responsibility were the specific character strengths that correlated most strongly with well-being and resiliency. For other kids, however, kindness, generosity, optimism, and spirituality correlated most strongly with positive life outcomes. In other words, it isn't "one size fits all" when it comes to identifying the most important character strengths for your gifted child! What was indisputable, however, was that character strengths should become an integral component in a triple package of *heart strengths!*

What we did find was that all gifted kids benefit from learning to be more patient, kind, empathic and compassionate, flexible, and open-minded. And that all gifted kids also benefit from learning to be more adaptable, self-confident, organized, good-natured, and generous. No big surprise here! As a parent, you might want to explore four or five *signature character strengths* beneficial for your child.

In my work with parents, I use a list of about 60 character strength adjectives that includes the following words: *adaptable, affectionate, appreciative, calm, cheerful, compassionate, considerate, cooperative, determined, eager, easygoing, empathic, enthusiastic, flexible, friendly, generous, gentle, good-natured, helpful, hopeful, industrious, kind, likeable, loving and lovable, loyal, modest, open-minded, outgoing, patient, prudent, reflective, relaxed, responsible, self-confident, sincere, sociable, spiritual, spontaneous, sympathetic, tenacious, thoughtful, tolerant, trusting, and warm.* I share the list and ask each parent to circle no more than ten adjectives from the list that characterizes their son or daughter's *signature strengths.* Then I ask the parents to go back and circle five-or-six adjectives denoting character strengths that they'd like to see their son or daughter further strengthen. This becomes our starting point for discussing ways to strengthen these character strengths. For each family, the list of adjectives we focus on is slightly different. Please feel free to use the above list of adjectives or create your own list to use with your family!

General Tips on Promoting Character Strengths

The VIA Institute of Character is a nonprofit organization with the mission to advance the science and practice of character development. The organization is easy to access online at: www.viacharacter.org. The VIA Institute offers online courses, free articles and videos on character development, and personalized coaching. Particularly relevant to our discussion here, they offer a free online survey of character strengths for adults and for kids, ages 8–12. Anyone can register, at no cost, to take their character strengths survey. The Institute provides free feedback after you or your child completes their online survey. The survey includes questions like: *"I work really well in a group"* and *"I am always kind to other kids."* Each survey question includes five possible answers ranging from *"very much unlike me"* to *"very much like me."*

The beauty of the *VIA Character Strengths Scale* is that it provides parents with an easily accessible profile of your daughter or son's *signature character strengths* (and weaknesses). I've invited parents in my consulting practice and at workshops to complete the online VIA Survey and have their child complete the VIA Youth Survey— and then share the results that The VIA Institute provides for our exploration. The results are an excellent starting point and benchmark for parents to guide building new or strengthening fledging character strengths with their child.

Character traits are not inborn, although there is evidence that, like most human traits, they are influenced by genes. The good news is that character strengths can be learned and perfected with practice. Many character strengths serve as valuable antidotes for gifted kids who can appear as obnoxious, entitled, overly competitive, self-centered, individualistic, self-absorbed, self-promoting, even narcissistic and cruel (Post, 2022). The ability to empathize, demonstrate compassion, be kind, humble, appreciative, optimistic, tactful, generous, calm, and sympathetic predicts future life success, positive physical and mental health, and authentic happiness.

Michele Borba is a parenting expert and author of a highly readable paperback, *Thrivers: The Surprising Reasons Why Some Kids Struggle and Others Shine* (2022). Borba points out two things that separate successful kids from what she calls "*the herd*": having at least one caring, involved parent in your child's life, and teaching your child seven essential character strengths—what she calls *the seven essential virtues*: self-confidence, empathy, self-control, integrity, curiosity, perseverance, and optimism. Borba believes that these character strengths optimize kids' potential and what she calls their "thriving abilities."

Family Meetings

Recall from the previous chapter that I recommend *family meetings* as an excellent forum to teach your child the many skills underlying strengths of the heart. Build family meetings into your weekly family schedule! Family meetings provide a distinctive, relaxed, comfortable, and open-minded venue which supports nonthreatening and tolerant dialogue among family members. Family meetings are a wonderful opportunity for parents to talk about and demonstrate character strengths—what they are, why they are important, and how your gifted child can grow them. The same is true about Emotional Intelligence and social skills.

Essentially, family meetings promote family harmony, respect, improved communication, family intimacy, and new social-emotional skills. Successful family meetings don't have to last very long. They should never become tedious, mind-numbing, monotonous, or God-forbid, aversive. I have found that it's easier to start the family meeting after an early dinner but before the kids run off to do homework (or watch YouTube, play video games, or text friends!). A period of 20–30 minutes, once or twice a week, seems to be a doable for most 21st century families! Some meetings should be guided by an agenda—for example, if the kids or parents have a gripe or concern that they want to discuss openly as a family. For example, your adolescent may want to petition to discuss relaxing her curfew or her desire to take public transportation to school. Or your child may want you to discontinue checking her homework. You get the idea! Almost any topic is fair game for discussion at family meetings. Some family meetings can be agenda free. These are perfect opportunities to discuss one character strength that you'd like your child to work on refining. Family meetings are also an excellent opportunity to talk about emotions. Or talk about social skills.

At family meetings, you can discuss any of the character strengths from my adjective checklist above, or the VIA Youth Survey as worth digging deeper into with your child. There really is an almost inexhaustible number of ways to creatively talk with your kids at family meetings about kindness, teamwork, sharing, gratitude, fairness, humility, kindness, gratitude, compassion, tact, honesty, enthusiasm and passion, forgiveness, and playfulness. Be ingenious. You can bring in film, TV shows, books, puppets, role plays, and actual examples from family, school or neighborhood, or current events to make more concrete and underscore the lesson.

Family meetings are wonderful opportunities for parents to teach their kids about emotions. They are a perfect venue to help them build a vocabulary of emotions by naming emotions in real time. During family meetings, share your own emotions so that your child feels safe sharing theirs. Ask your child if they have observed how other kids in their class are feeling and then discuss how they came to make that determination. This is what is called teaching *emotional literacy*. The same is true in teaching social skills at family meetings. The family meeting is the perfect venue to discuss, demonstrate, and practice taking turns, listening before speaking, not interrupting when another family member is speaking, being polite, and having good table manners. The list of social skills that you can teach and reinforce during family meetings is almost infinite!

Journaling

Journaling is another way that you can help your gifted child build character strength. I routinely use journaling with parents and gifted kids to emphasize the power of the character strength, *gratitude*. Research indicates that keeping a *daily gratitude journal* for at least two weeks leads to significant positive outcomes! At family meetings, I encourage clients to take a few moments to go around the kitchen table to each share one, two, or three things that they are thankful for. This simple character strength building activity may sound schmalzy or contrived. But families love its simplicity and power. Building gratitude works! And gratitude is deeply embedded in and has its roots in ancient philosophy and religion. The Roman statesman Cicero purportedly called gratitude not only the greatest but the parent virtue.

Remember my recommendation from Chapter 2 to model the kinds of behaviors that you want your kids to learn. Get in the habit of talking to your kids about *why* good things happen to you and to them, and your appreciation for the people responsible for making the good things happen. Help your child to better regulate negative emotions and become calmer and more composed by demonstrating being a calm problem solver.

Bibliotherapy

Using literature to build character strengths is another technique that works. We call it *bibliotherapy*. One self-help book for bright teens who enjoy reading and like to use books to learn is, *What Do You Stand For? A Guide to Building Character* (2005). The author is Barbara Lewis. The book is also a great read for parents! The book is listed in the suggested resources at the end of this chapter. There are innumerable short stories and books, written as fables, with animals as characters, designed to teach cultural values. Fables come with wonderful moral lessons! Three examples are, *"slow and steady wins the race;" "a kindness is never wasted,"* and *"the flatterer lives at the expense of those who listen to him."* Young kids and older kids (and adults) can learn much about character strengths from reading and discussing these wonderful and often humorous allegories. Fables explore optimism, empathy, compassion, patience, gratitude, kindness, honesty, cooperation, and teamwork. The very character strengths that we are talking about!

Concluding Comments

This chapter highlights the importance of character strengths. Character strengths are universal and recognized by most cultural anthropologists and historians as essential to the survival of our species. Like social skills and Emotional Intelligence, character strengths are crucial interpersonal skills and traits that are first learned in the home by your young child observing how you, their parent, behaves. Very early in life, character strengths are learned without any formal or intentional teaching by parents and others in the home. Character strengths are later learned by purposeful instruction from the parent in the home, by teachers in the classroom, in Sunday School and religious programs, at social clubs, and when participating in youth athletic and social organizations. Athletic coaches and group leaders in the community, music, dance, art, theater, gymnastics, cooking class, and martial arts instructors are all potentially important role models demonstrating good (or not-so-good) character strengths. Readers can probably think of at least one upsetting, painful, or even agonizing personal story about some adult in your own life or in your child's life who was a dreadful role model. Many adults, sadly, fall short of demonstrating admirable character strength.

A lack of character strength—even at an early age, can cause your otherwise smart child to become obnoxious, entitled, overly competitive, self-centered, highly individualistic, uncooperative, self-absorbed, self-promoting, and even narcissistic and cruel. In other words, character strengths, just like social skills and Emotional Intelligence, are important! The good news is that character strengths can be learned and perfected with practice. Many character strengths serve as valuable antidotes for today's ills. The ability to empathize, be compassionate, kind, humble, appreciative, optimistic, tactful, generous, calm, and sympathetic predicts future life success, physical and mental health, and authentic happiness.

Character strengths are one of the three pillars of the *strengths of the heart* model. Sadly, all too often, parents and teachers mistakenly assume that kids, including gifted kids, learn *heart strengths* implicitly, tacitly, or subliminally. That they don't need to have them taught. This is not true! Too many bright kids are not so bright about character strengths. They need to learn them to be successful in life.

Suggested Resources

Bennett, W. J. (1995). *The children's book of virtues.* New York: Simon & Schuster.

Borba, M. (2021). *Thrivers: The surprising reasons why some kids struggle and others shine.* New York: Penguin Random House.

Campbell, M. (2018) *Adrian Simcox does not have a horse.* New York: Penguin Books.

Case, J. (2017). *Emma and the whale.* New York: Penguin Books.

de la Peña, M. (2015). *Last stop on Market Street.* New York: Penguin Books.

Doerrfeld, C. (2018). *The rabbit listened.* New York: Penguin Books.

Eyre, L., & Eyre, R. (1993). *Teaching your children values.* New York: Simon & Schuster.

Henn, S. (2017). *Pass it on.* New York: Penguin Books.

Hoose, P. & House, H. (1998). *Hey, little ant.* New York: Random House.

LeBox, A. (2015). *Peace is an offering.* New York: Penguin Books.

Lewis, B. A. (2005). *What do you stand for? For teens. A guide to building character*. Minneapolis, MN: Free Spirit Publishing.

McGhee, H. M. (2017). *Come with me*. New York: Penguin Books.

Palacio, R. J. (2017). *We're all wonders*. New York: Penguin Books.

Roberts, J. (2014). *The smallest girl in the smallest grade*. New York: Penguin Books.

Unell, B. C., & Wyckoff, J. L. (1995). *20 Teachable virtues: Practical ways to pass on lessons of virtue and character to your children*. New York: A Pedigree Book.

Vere, E. (2018). *How to be a lion*. New York: Penguin Books.

VIA Institute on Character: www.viacharacter.org

Woodson, J. (2012). *Each kindness*. New York: Penguin Books.

Zaki, J. (2019). *The war for kindness: Building empathy in a fractured world*. New York: Crown.

References

Borba, M. (2021). *Thrivers: The surprising reasons why some kids struggle and others shine*. New York: Penguin Random House.

Darling-Hammond, L. (2015). Social and emotional learning. Critical skills for building healthy schools. In J. A. Durlak, C. E. Domitrovich, R. P. Weissberg, & T. P. Gullotta (Eds.), *Handbook of social and emotional learning: Research and practice* (pp. xi–xiii). New York: Guilford.

Durkak, J. A., Domitrovich, C. E., Weissberg, R. P., & Gullotta, T. P. (Eds.) (2015). *Handbook of social and emotional learning: Research and practice*. New York: The Guilford Press.

Jones, D. E., Greenberg, M., & Crowley, M. (2015). Early social-emotional functioning and public health: The relationship between kindergarten social competence and future wellness. *American Journal of Public Health, 195*, 2283–2290.

Lewis, B. A. (2005). *What do you stand for? A guide to building character*. Minneapolis, MN: Free Spirit.

Peterson, C., & Seligman, M. E. P. (2004). *Character strengths and virtues: A handbook and classification*. Oxford: Oxford University Press.

Pfeiffer, S. I. (2017). Success in the classroom and in life: Focusing on strengths of the head and strengths of the heart. *Gifted Education International, 33*, 95–101.

Pfeiffer, S. I., & Blankenship, A. P. (2017). Lessons learned from working with highly gifted and creative kids. *Psychology and Education, 54*, 24–32.

Post, G. (2022). *The gifted parenting journey*. Goshen, KY: Gifted Unlimited.

Suldo, S. M., Hearon, B. V., & Shaughness-Dedrick, E. (2018). Examining gifted students' mental health through the lens of positive psychology. In S. I. Pfeiffer (Ed.). *APA handbook of giftedness and talent* (pp. 433–449). Washington, DC: American Psychological Association Books.

Weissberg, R. P., Durlak, J. A., Domitrovich, C. E., & Gullotta, T. P. (2015). Social and emotional learning: Past, present, and future. In J. A. Durlak, C. E. Domitrovich, R. P. Weissberg, & T. P. Gullotta (Eds.), *Handbook of social and emotional learning. Research and Practice* (pp. 3–19). New York: Guilford Press.

6

Social Skills Make a Difference

Frederick Douglas once said "It is easier to build strong children than to repair broken men" (1845). Keep this in mind as we explore social skills below.

What Are Social Skills?

As a reminder, my model *strengths of the heart* consist of three components: social skills, Emotional Intelligence, and character strengths. In this chapter, I briefly discuss the last of these three components, social skills. What they are. Why they are important. And how parents can intentionally teach and reinforce them.

A social skill is a skill, proficiency, knack, or competence that promotes or facilitates interaction and communication with others—it can be verbal or nonverbal. The process of your child learning these varied and important social skills over their lifetime is called socialization. These vital life skills are often learned by your child simply by

DOI: 10.4324/9781003287070-6

watching how their social world operates, without any formal or intentional teaching. We talked about this earlier in the book when I mentioned how important it is for you, as a parent, to model socially appropriate behavior. Remember that your gifted child learns what she or he observes!

Social skills are also learned early in life by purposeful instruction from you and your partner, from their grandparents and other relatives, from older siblings, and later, by teachers and other significant adults in their lives. Social skills are taught in their classrooms, in Sunday School and religious programs, at social clubs and scouting organizations such as Brownies, Cub Scouts, Campfire Girls, and 4H clubs, and even when your child is participating on youth athletic teams. You get my point. Opportunities for learning social skills are all around us! A lack of social skills—even at an early age, can create for your child social awkwardness, peer relation problems, low self-esteem, victimization, depression, and behavior problems.

Social skills are essential interpersonal tools that enable your child to communicate, interact, learn, ask for help, support, or clarification, and get their needs met in appropriate ways. Social skills are the tools that allow your child to get along with others, make friends, and develop age-appropriate, healthy relationships—with both peers and adults.

Any deficits in your child's social skills can be perilous and create huge problems for your child. Social skill deficits can result from many different factors, for example, your child may not know how to compromise, apologize, develop give-and-take relationships, graciously accept failure or defeat, or cope with rejection or disappointment (Coleman, Pfeiffer, & Oakland, 1992; Dowd & Tierney, 2017). Many bright kids simply don't have in their repertoire these important, age-appropriate social skills. They never learned them.

Social skill deficits can also be the result of your child being overly anxious or depressed, or having a neuro-atypical developmental problem, such as autism spectrum disorder or ADHD. Anxiety, depression, and neurodevelopmental conditions can compromise a child's ability to know exactly how, when, or why to enact a set of social skills in a given situation. I often encounter these social skill challenges—social skill deficits and social skill dysfluencies, in my clinical practice when working with high ability kids with coexisting psychological disorders (Pfeiffer & Foley Nicpon, 2018). The important take-home point is that social skills are critically important for your child to learn and be comfortable and fluent enacting. And be able to recognize the right time and place and social situation to use them!

Why Social Skills Matter

Social skills are essential to your child's success in life. Social skills allow your child to effectively communicate with you and with others. Social skills allow your child to connect with peers and adults in their world. Social skills make it easier for your child to make friends, get along with siblings and classmates, and cooperate in the give-and-take social world that we all live in. Social skills are the building blocks for your kid's ongoing cognitive development and for their vibrant mental health.

Social skills are the building blocks for Emotional Intelligence—what we earlier covered. And social skills are the building blocks for character strengths—what we discussed in the last chapter. We are social animals. Functioning in your family, and in their school, community, and the larger society require that your gifted child be proficient in a great many social skills. Social skills get more complex and more nuanced as your child gets older. And yet, these days a great many bright kids and adolescents spend long hours alone, staring at the screens of digital devices, playing virtual games in their room, missing opportunities to hone important, positive social and interpersonal skills! We know that social skills are one of the most important set of competencies that kids and adolescents need to develop. Along with Emotional Intelligence and character strengths, they predict to future life success, well-being, vibrant mental health, and resiliency (Robert Wood Johnson Foundation, 2015).

The reader is by now aware of how essential good social skills are to your child's ability to get along with others, make and sustain friendships, be well-liked, and deal with life's disappointments and stresses. The science of human resiliency has demonstrated, over the last 30 years, that youngsters and adults require, over the course of their lifetime, culturally sensitive and developmentally appropriate social skills. They are that important.

There are literally hundreds of social skills that I could provide you with as examples of quintessential, *signature social skills* for your child to learn. To make my point, I'll restrict my list to a *"Baker's Dozen."*[1] These are examples of social skills that I often find myself working on with gifted kids in counseling. I am confident that you can generate your own list of vital, *signature social skills* from your own experience growing up. And from your experience as a parent! Okay, here is my *Baker's Dozen* important social skills that gifted kids need to learn:

- ◆ thinking before speaking or acting;
- ◆ accepting consequences graciously;
- ◆ helping other kids and adults;
- ◆ waiting patiently;
- ◆ courteously accepting criticism;
- ◆ resisting peer pressure;
- ◆ being polite and using good manners;
- ◆ being a good sport and good loser;
- ◆ understanding humor and how not to offend others;
- ◆ avoiding bullies and kids in cliquey groups;
- ◆ being a good listener;
- ◆ knowing how and when to compromise; and
- ◆ respecting other kids' personal space.

General Tips on Promoting Social Skills

In addition to counseling, there are many ways that kids with social skill deficits can learn social skills. One popular way of teaching social skills is using self-help books—what we psychologists call bibliotherapy. Barbara Cooper and Nancy Widdows (2008) authored a nifty paperback that consists of 40 skill-building activities for teens who would benefit from strengthening their social-skills. The authors state that they wrote their self-help book for adolescents with nonverbal learning disorders, Asperger's, and "other social-skill problems." I've used this book in my practice with adolescents who are willing to practice the activities at home and then review their work with me or with their parents. Examples of the social skill training activities in the book include: *Things that make me worry; Things that make me angry; Different points of view; When I am angry; Changing the plan in my head; Cool-down tools: Deep breaths; Cool-down tools: Drawing and writing; Go with the flow; Creating new self-talk; Conversation skills; Choosing your friends; Shades of gray; and The unwritten rules of life.*

The 40 activities are arranged sequentially in the workbook to build upon one another. All the activities include opportunities for your child or adolescent to write a story, jot down feelings or examples from their own life, create a collage, drawing, or poem, share personal experiences, or create a cartoon. Kids enjoy the activities and discussing each of the social skill lessons embedded within each activity. I've used this book with gifted kids as young as 8–10.

Another popular self-help book written for kids on building social skills is *Growing Friendships: A kids' guide to making and keeping friends*, by Eileen Kennedy-Moore and Christine McLaughlin (2017). Bright kids enjoy the book's lighthearted, humorous style and cartoons. But make no mistake, the important and practical social-skills lessons provided in this self-help book are research-based and work. In my practice, gifted kids as young as 7 and as old as 18 have benefited from practicing the important social-skills lessons offered in the book.

The book by Kennedy-Moore and McLaughlin addresses many thorny social-skills challenges. The authors provide case studies and personal stories that illustrate many common social challenges. Instead of providing activities, the book includes easy-to-follow comics. Examples of some of the social challenges that the book tackles are: *How to deal with kids who feel alone, ineffectually try to impress others, cry easily, criticize others, are reluctant to participate and "stand on the sidelines," are afraid of not being the best, give in to others too much, overreact to teasing, hold grudges, and act like "a sore loser."* The book is appropriate for gifted kids ages 6 to 12 years old.

Both books, *A Kids' Guide to Making and Keeping Friend*s, and, *The Social Success Workbook for Teens*, by Cooper and Widdows, are popular self-help books that I recommend to bright kids who would benefit from improving their social skills.

A book that I recommend for parents and adolescents is: *Social Rules for Kids: The Top 100 Social Rules Kids Need to Succeed* (2011). The author is Susan Diamond. This paperback offers 100 social rules; Susan Diamond suggests that one to three social rules from her list of 100 can easily be taught per week and practiced daily. The book is designed to facilitate conversation and fun activities that parents and kids can work on together. Several scenarios include fun role-playing activities, which provide opportunities to put the newly learned social skills to the test.

Family Meetings

I recommend that parents work together with their kids on no more than two of the 100 social rules activities with their kids during any given family meeting. As you know, I strongly encourage, in my consulting practice, parents schedule weekly *family meetings* with their children. Family meetings establish a unique, nonjudgmental venue that supports an open and nonthreatening dialogue among all family members. Family meetings are a wonderful opportunity for parents to teach social skills (and learn more about their kids!). Details about running a family meeting can be found in the previous two chapters. Essentially, family meetings are designed to promote family harmony, respect, improved communication, and intimacy.

Family meetings work best when the family meets regularly—perhaps once or twice weekly, at the same time and place to build a positive family tradition. No cell phones are allowed at family meetings, everyone needs to practice "active listening" and using "I" messages, and all family members should be encouraged to participate. I should point out that family meetings are an excellent format for parents to teach all three of the heart strengths: Emotional Intelligence, character strengths, and social skills!

Five examples from the 100 social rules in Susan Diamond's book that are easily discussed at family meetings are: *"Remember: Everyone get a turn to talk, and we keep the ball going"*; *"Remember: If I disagree with my friend (or parent or teacher's answer), it is okay. Not everyone thinks the way I think"*; *"Remember: Everyone gets a chance to choose, and we compromise because we want to have friends"*; *"Remember: Being a tattle-tale is not okay"*; and *"Remember: Kids will not want to play with me if I am a bad sport."*

Concluding Comments

This chapter highlights that social skills promote and facilitate interaction and communication with others. These crucial skills are often learned by kids watching how their social world operates, without any formal or intentional teaching by parents or others.

Social skills are also learned early in life by purposeful instruction from the parent and others in their social world. Social skills are taught in the classroom, in Sunday School and religious programs, at social clubs and scouting organizations such as Brownies, Cub Scouts, Campfire Girls, and 4H clubs, and when participating in youth athletic programs. A lack of social skills—even at an early age, creates social awkwardness, peer relation problems, low self-esteem, victimization, depression, and behavior problems for gifted kids. In other words, social skills are important!

Social skills are one of the three pillars of the *strengths of the heart* model. Sadly, all too often, parents and teachers mistakenly assume that gifted kids learn social skills implicitly, tacitly, or subliminally. And don't need to be taught them. This is not necessarily true! Some gifted kids are far from knowledgeable about age-appropriate social skills. They need to learn them to be successful in life. And there are even some gifted kids, for a variety of reasons, who are uncomfortable or unsavvy communicating or demonstrating age-appropriate social skills. For example, they may be excessively shy, anxious, or depressed, and benefit from direct consultation with a psychologist or counselor.

Check out the **Suggested Resources** at the end of this chapter. You will find a number self-help books written for parents and for kids on social skills training. There are even self-help books on how kids can learn etiquette: For example, see Katherine Flannery's book, *A Kids' Guide to Manners* below.

Suggested Resources

Bowers, M. (2015). *8 keys to raising the quirky child: How to help a kid who doesn't (quite) fit in.* New York: W. W. Norton.

Cooper, B., & Widdows, N. (2008). *Social success workbook for teens.* Oakland, CA: New Harbinger Publications.

Daniels, N. (2019). *Social skills activities for kids: 50 fun exercises for making friends, talking and listening, and understanding social rules.* Emeryville, CA: Rockridge Press.

Diamond, S. (2011). *Social rules for kids: The top 100 social rules kids need to succeed.* Shawnee Mission, KS: AAPC Publishing.

Flannery, K. (2018). *A kids' guide to manners: 50 fun etiquette lessons for kids* (and their families). Emeryville, CA: Rockridge Press.

Ford Inman, T., & Kirchner, J. (2016). *Parenting gifted children 101: An introduction to gifted kids and their needs.* Waco, TX: Prufrock Press.

Kennedy-Moore, E., & McLaughlin, C. (2017). *Growing friendships: A kids guide to making and keeping friends.* New York: Aladdin.

Pfeiffer, S. I. (2003). Psychological considerations in raising a healthy gifted child. In P. Olszewski-Kubilius, L. Limburg-Weber, & S. I. Pfeiffer (Eds.). *Early gifts: Recognizing and nurturing children's talents* (pp. 173–185). Waco, TX: Prufrock Press.

Shapiro, L. E., & Holmes, J. (2008). *Let's be friends. A workbook to help kids learn social skills and make great friends.* Oakland, CA: New Harbinger Publications.

Siegel, D. (2011). *Mindsight: Transform your brain with the new science of kindness.* San Francisco, CA: Berrett-Koehle

Note

1 I refer to a *Baker's Dozen* a few times in this pocketbook! Truth be told, I worked in a local bakery during my high school days, and obviously I was favorably affected by this early job experience!

References

Coleman, M., Pfeiffer, S. I., & Oakland, T. (1992). Aggression replacement training with behaviorally disordered adolescents. *Behavioral Disorders, 18,* 54–66.

Cooper, B., & Widdows, N. (2008). *Social success workbook for teens.* Oakland, CA: New Harbinger Publications.

Diamond, S. (2011). *Social rules for kids: The top 100 social rules kids need to succeed.* Shawnee Mission, KS: AAPC Publishing.

Douglass, F. (1845, 2009). *Narrative of the life of Frederick Douglass, an American Slave.* Oxford: Oxford University Press.

Dowd, T. P., & Tierney, J. (2017). *Teaching social skills to youth: A step-by-step guide to 182 basic to complex skills plus helpful teaching techniques.* Omaha, NE: Boys Town Press.

Kennedy-Moore, E., & McLaughlin, C. (2017). *Growing friendships: A kids guide to making and keeping friends.* New York: Aladdin.

Pfeiffer, S. I., & Foley-Nicpon, M. (2018). Knowns and unknowns about students with disabilities who also happen to be intellectually gifted. In Scott Barry Kaufman (Ed.), *Twice exceptional: Supporting and education bright and creative students with learning disabilities* (pp. 104–121). New York: Oxford University Press.

Robert Wood Johnson Foundation (2015). *How children's social skills impact success in adulthood: Findings from a 20-year study on the outcomes of children screened in kindergarten.* Retrieved April 16, 2021, from https://eric.ed.gov/?id=ED592871

7

Frequently Asked Questions by Parents

When considering frequently asked questions I'm reminded of the American theoretical physicist and Philosopher Sean M. Carroll who once said "Science isn't just about solving this or that puzzle. It's about understanding how the world works ..."

This chapter presents three frequently asked questions by parents of gifted kids. And my answers to each of the three popular questions. I have adopted a style in answering each of the questions that I typically use when conversing with a parent, consulting with a colleague, teacher, psychologist, or pediatrician, standing in front of an audience at a parent workshop, or responding to an e-mail from a concerned parent. In other words, my answers are intentionally *not* written in an academic or professorial style. I have tried to minimize research citations because that is not how I typically respond in the real world to questions from parents, educators, the media, and others. Okay, here goes. I hope that you find the questions relevant to your

DOI: 10.4324/9781003287070-7

own parenting experience. And I hope that you find the answers helpful and instructive!

What Is the Impact of Giftedness on My Child's Psychological Well-being?

The good news is that gifted kids as a group—at least kids who are intellectually or academically precocious, are no more likely—to have social, emotional, or behavioral problems than their nongifted peers. Unfortunately, we don't have much research or hard data on the psychological well-being and vulnerabilities of young kids or prodigies with uncanny gifts in the fields of music, dance, theater, athletics, or other nonacademic domains. There is a lot of opinion! But no hard research.

As a group, gifted kids are at no greater risk. This is the good news. Most of the gifted kids that I've had the pleasure of working with at Duke, at the Florida Governor's School for Science and Space Technology, and in my private practice were well-adjusted and did not appear as weird, nerdy, or brainiacs. However, this does not mean that *all* gifted kids are without quirks. This does not mean that *all* gifted kids enjoy robust and hardy psychological well-being, happiness, success, and joy in life. That would not be true. As I will mention in a second, some gifted kids suffer from psychological and behavioral problems. Such as depression, excessive fears and anxiety, an eating disorder, poor impulse control and undue aggression, and other psychiatric disorders. Some gifted kids endure extreme moodiness, frequent meltdowns, negative perfectionism, overexcitability, and agonizing stubbornness.

These are the kind of problems that bring parents to my consulting office!

However, not all the problems that gifted kids suffer from are full-blown psychiatric disorders. Some are what we call subclinical problems that can worsen and become more serious or lessen and resolve with counseling. And some are not psychiatric problems at all but are rather deficits in age-appropriate social skills, Emotional Intelligence, or character strength—problems with undeveloped or under-developed *strengths of the heart!*

Some authorities in the gifted field suggest that gifted kids, because of their advanced thinking and problem-solving abilities—what we now call superior executive functioning, may be more resilient and better prepared to successfully cope with life's challenges and stressors. There is not a whole lot of research evidence supporting this theory. Or refuting it, for that matter. That said, I've seen in my work at Duke and at the Florida Governor's School, and in my clinical practice some very smart kids adept at getting along with others, handling stress, solving social problems, and resolving conflicts. Smart kids who are well-adjusted and free of mental health issues.

We do know that gifted kids make up an extremely diverse group! Within this great diversity, some subgroups of gifted kids are certainly at heightened risk for psycho-social and emotional difficulties. Let me take a moment to speak about a few of these subgroups at increased risk. In my experience, there are at least five subgroups:

1. First, there are **gifted kids whose gifts—be it intellectual, academic or in any culturally valued domain—go unrecognized or unmet.** This subgroup

of gifted whose gifts are ignored, undervalued, or discounted, are at risk for negative and untoward psychological consequences.

2. **Second, there are some gifted kids who have difficulty making friends and feel a pressure to act "normal," who downplay or disguise their gifts.** All too often, gifted kids conceal or mask their special gifts. In their attempt to fit in and be accepted by their peers, they "dummy down." Interestingly enough, we don't see this phenomenon among gifted kids in the performing arts or athletics.

3. **Third, there are a subset of very highly gifted kids who are super-bright or super-talented.** These super-outstanding gifted kids often have difficulty fitting in, finding other peers who they can relate to. This subgroup, by the very nature of the relative rarity of their lofty gifts, are at increased risk for psychosocial and emotional difficulties.

4. **Fourth, there are gifted kids of color, from immigrant families or minority ethnic or religious groups, of a different sexual identity or orientation, living in poverty or a dangerous neighborhood, and/or with a developmental, physical, or mental disability.** Any of these factors put this subgroup of gifted kids at heightened risk for mental health problems and adverse psychological well-being (Davis, 2022; Pfeiffer, 2013).

5. Finally, the fifth subgroup at risk for unfavorable outcomes are those **gifted kids lacking age-appropriate social skills, well-honed Emotional Intelligence, or cultivated character strength**—essentially, problems with *undeveloped, underdeveloped, or underutilized strengths of the heart.*

By now, the reader is familiar with my ideas about *strengths of the heart* and are authorities on the topic!

What Can We Parents Do to Ensure That Our Gifted Child Is Successful?

This is a question that most parents, at some point in their experience raising children, including parents of special needs kids, ask. My wife and I certainly asked it when we were raising our three children—now all grown adults with kids of their own! There are, of course, a great many parenting self-help books on the topic. Some are quite good. In my private practice, I often recommend to parents one of the following self-help books, all listed in the **Suggested Resources** section at the end of the chapter:

- ◆ *The Optimistic Child*, by Martin Seligman
- ◆ *Kid Confidence*, by Eileen Kennedy-Moore
- ◆ *Smart Parenting for Smart Kids*, by Eileen Kennedy-Moore
- ◆ *Parenting Gifted Children 101: An Introduction to Gifted Kids and Their Needs*, by Tracy Inman.
- ◆ *Parenting from the Inside Out*, by Daniel Siegel and Mary Hartzell

I also often provide parents a sixth option: a copy of a chapter which I wrote titled: "Psychological considerations in raising a healthy gifted child" or a copy of my book *Serving the Gifted*.[1] In the chapter and in my book, I offer four suggestions that I believe help create family harmony and encourage *strengths of the heart*. The four suggestions are: *promote balance in your gifted child's life*; *normalize your*

*gifted child's experiences; set and enforce age-appropriate rules
and limits;* and *promote your gifted child's character and social
intelligence.*

Promoting balance in your gifted child's life means that
you need to protect your child and yourself from getting
caught up in excessively focusing on your child's special
gifts or talents to the relative neglect of other important
social, emotional, and developmental experiences. Of
course, nurturing your child's special talents are important
and many would argue, a parent's responsibility. However,
the danger is letting the scales tip to place excessive or too
much emphasis—in terms of time, mental energy, travel,
rearranged family schedules, family resources, and the
like—on promoting your child's special gift. What can
happen is that your gifted child inadvertently misses out on
other important socialization experiences. In other words,
sometimes—and I emphasize *sometimes!*—too much of a
good thing in pursuit of developing your son or daughter's
special talent—tutoring, private lessons, excessive practice, special classes, after-school programs, summer camps,
online courses, competitions—can be detrimental to your
child's overall psychological health and well-being.

Normalize your gifted child's experiences, the second
suggestion, means this: provide and make available to your
gifted child or adolescent a range of social activities and
experiences that are *both* age and developmentally appropriate. The challenge becomes taking on *double duty* since
gifted kids' pattern of strengths and weaknesses tend to
be more varied and divergent than for normal kids. Gifted
kids benefit from exposure to normalizing experiences that
include activities and social experiences that are clearly
advanced, if parents expect to match their child's precocious gifts with activities that challenge and engage them!

At the same time, gifted kids benefit from normalizing experiences that are age-appropriate, since even highly gifted kids are still kids and not necessarily advanced in all spheres of their life. Pragmatically, this means that your gifted kid benefits from opportunities to interact with other equally gifted peers who share similar interests. This is important for their developing identity, self-esteem, overall comfort, and *head strengths*. And gifted kids also need opportunities to interact with their same-age peers.

Set and enforce age-appropriate rules and limits may sound like a rather conventional and even conservative recommendation. And it really is! I admit that, at heart, I am both a liberal progressivist and a traditionalist. Hey, I spent seven years in the military—as an officer and clinical psychologist! I respect civil, courteous, considerate, thoughtful, and kind behaviors. I believe that good manners and respect for others—even those we disagree with, makes a huge difference in promoting a more gentle, compassionate, generous, and charitable community. Including the family community.

In my experience, I have observed that all kids benefit and thrive when they are raised in families (and in schools) that include clearly stated limits, rules, and expectations for acceptable behavior and conduct. All kids (including gifted kids) need limits because limits are instrumental in teaching appropriate behavior, in communicating a sense of security and community, and in conveying parental care, love, and concern. Rules and limits learned early within the family help gifted kids to get along with others outside of the home, develop and maintain friendships, deal effectively with conflicts and disappointments, and appreciate that they are part of a larger social world. Rules, limits, and discipline applied in a fair, consistent, and a loving way promote empathy and compassion. And inoculate gifted kids from developing selfish, conceited, and even narcissistic tendencies.

Some authorities in the gifted field suggest that high IQ kids need fewer constraints or rules than others. There is absolutely no evidence to support this radical and dangerous position. As a parent, it is tempting to think that your gifted kid has better judgment and is more socially mature than other kids his or her own age—a tempting thought, for sure. But there is no research supporting this view! In my clinical practice, I have worked with parents who have embraced a *laissez-faire* or even hands-off approach to disciplining their gifted child. The result, all-too-often, is an ill-mannered, poorly disciplined, self-absorbed, and selfish gifted child or adolescent with peer relation and authority issues.

My recommendation to parents is to establish clear, consistent, flexible family rules. Kids, including gifted kids, often test limits. It is perfectly normal to expect your gifted child to challenge family rules. Gifted kids are particularly curious in wanting to understand your rationale for each rule, what you will do if they push the limits or break the rule, and whether you will be consistent in enforcing a rule. So be prepared to explain family rules at *family meetings*.

Promote your gifted child's character and social intelligence is the fourth suggestion that I often share with parents. This recommendation should come as no surprise to readers. It is the essence and soul of my commitment to *strengths of the heart*! As you by now know, I am a huge advocate for encouraging your gifted child's social intelligence. So that your child understands and develops the social and interpersonal skills to be courteous, a good listener, likeable, helpful, trustworthy, a *team player*, and able to get along with others—other kids and adults. *Social intelligence*, you may remember, overlaps with *Emotional Intelligence*, social maturity, and *character strength*. Simply stated, helping your gifted kid develop their *social skills* and *social intelligence* will increase the likelihood that they will enjoy a rich, satisfying, and successful life!

Gifted kids with well-developed *social intelligence* are at ease with peers and adults, including nongifted peers. They are quietly self-confident but not conceited or condescending, and adept at handling stressful interpersonal situations at home, in the classroom, on the playground, and in the neighborhood. They are friendly and comfortable *in their skin*, almost as if they have watched a YouTube video by Dale Carnegie, *How to make friends and influence people.* As I have explained in earlier chapters, young kids, including gifted kids, do not come into the world knowing these important *soft people skills*. Even super-bright kids need to learn from their parents and others about virtuous habits, good manners, and culturally valued and age-appropriate social skills. This is what we mean by *character development.* The ingredients to help create *social intelligence* include setting a good example. Nothing is more impactful than teaching by quiet example. Make standards clear and expectations high, but not unreasonable. Using *family meetings* to discuss with your child right and wrong; the way the world works—often unfair—and the way people ought to live and treat one another and the planet. Finally, avoid rushing in to rescue your child when problems or conflicts arise. Help your gifted child develop problem-solving skills and the self-confidence and self-sufficiency to take the lead in resolving his or her own problems.

One final point bears mentioning. Remember that *Grandma's Rules* offers suggestions to promote parental well-being. We parents need to *have our acts together* if we hope to successfully promote our gifted child's *strengths of the heart* and success in life.

What about Suicide? Are Gifted Kids at Greater Risk or More Vulnerable for Suicide?

Suicide is a very serious mental health problem among adolescents and young adults. It is among the third leading cause of death among youth. More than 30,000 Americans commit suicide every year. Many thousands more try (Joiner, 2005). However, you should know that the rates of "successful suicides"—yes, I agree that this is a morbid term, a phrase which simply means those kids who end up dying as the result of a suicide attempt—are quite low in the general population. Approximately 4.5 per 100,000 (Hendin, et al., 2005). Considerable research and anecdotal evidence indicate that many more adolescents report having suicidal thoughts—called suicidal ideation, and suicidal gestures—not considered serious attempts but nonetheless quite distressing to their parents and friends (Cross, 2013).

Although there is widespread opinion, there is no published epidemiological research on the prevalence or incidence rates of suicide among gifted adolescents. The few studies that do exist suggest that there is no significant difference between the incidence of depression or suicide ideation for gifted and nongifted adolescents (Baker, 1995; Cross, 2013, Pfeiffer, 2013). My read of the scientific literature indicates that bright and gifted kids are at no greater or lesser risk for suicidal ideation, making a suicidal gesture, or attempting suicide. At the same time, I would be remiss not to share that some gifted kids think about suicide, make suicidal gestures, and attempt suicide.

Risk factors for all adolescents, including gifted kids, include untreated psychiatric disorders such as depression, anxiety, ADHD, and personality disorders; drug and alcohol abuse; family crisis or chronic dysfunction; significant peer relation problems, chronic teasing and bullying, and easy access to lethal methods (Cross, 2013; Davidson & Linnoila, 1991; Joiner, 2005; Pfeiffer & Stocking, 2000). My colleague at Florida State University, Thomas Joiner, is one of the leading experts on the psychology of suicide. Professor Joiner proposed his interpersonal theory of suicide. The theory explains why individuals engage in suicidal behavior. The interpersonal theory of suicide includes three operative components: the simultaneous presence of thwarted *belongingness*, perceived *burdensomeness*, and the ability to overcome one's *fear of death*. Several studies support Joiner's interpersonal theory of suicide, although I'm not aware of any research yet applying his theory to high IQ or gifted kids. I should point out that bright adolescents and young adults with well-developed social skills, advanced Emotional Intelligence, and potent character strengths—formidable *strengths of the heart*, are more likely to be resilient, optimistic, well-liked, successful, and psychologically healthy. In other words, *strengths of the heart* greatly reduce the risk of suicidal behavior.

Concluding Comments

These three questions are illustrative of the most frequently asked questions that I hear parents inquire about in private consultations and at parent workshops. My answers reflect how I typically respond to these questions. Of course, the three questions don't signify the many different questions that parents want answers to! In my book *Serving the Gifted*, you can find more parent questions and my opinions for each one.

In thinking about my career working with the gifted, I've heard many questions from sincere and concerned parents. Both in the USA and in my international travels. Space precludes me answering these many questions here. However, the resources listed at the end of this chapter offer insights into many. Please note that oftentimes at parent workshops, after hearing a personal question by a parent that seems to carry considerable personal distress, I privately take the parent aside and suggest that they might want to consult with a local mental health professional. Not all questions can be easily answered in a group format or in a book. Some questions are complex and nuanced and require professional guidance by a trained clinical counselor. There should never be any embarrassment in seeking consultation or counseling from a licensed mental health professional. What follows are a list of the questions that I have been most often asked by parents of gifted kids:

- ◆ In your experience, why do so many gifted kids underachieve?
- ◆ My husband and I are thinking about homeschooling our child. What are your thoughts about homeschooling gifted kids? Are there any risks we should be aware of?
- ◆ We've heard a lot about acceleration. Will accelerating my gifted kid put them at risk for social or emotional problems?

- Is there such a thing as gifted characteristics? We've heard about asynchrony and overexcitabilities and even perfectionism. And what about the stereotype of gifted nerds and social misfits? Are any of these characteristics true for all gifted kids?
- My husband and I would like to advocate for our gifted daughter. But we don't want our advocacy to be viewed or misinterpreted as pushy or overly aggressive parents. We know all about the "Tiger Mom"[2] and "Stage Mom" labels, and that's not us! Any suggestions?
- Our gifted son is very passionate, but also perhaps way too intense. He often over-reacts. Any recommendations on how to soften his intense personality?
- Are the gifted predisposed or more susceptible to emotional difficulties?
- How can we find support for parents of gifted kids? Do support groups exist like support groups for parents of kids with autism spectrum disorder or kids with ADHD?
- We just heard about Carol Dweck's theory of mindset. What can we do as parents to help our gifted child develop a growth mindset? Right now, our daughter is loath to take risks and seems to have a fixed mindset.
- Our gifted child doesn't get along well with his two siblings or with other children at school. Any suggestions?
- Our gifted child is so smart, but why does he act so immature? It drives my husband and I crazy!
- Is bullying and teasing a common problem among gifted kids? Our son is very bright but has

a difficult time making friends at his school and complains about being teased and bullied. Any advice?

◆ Might my wife and I be overly involved in our kid's schooling and after school activities? Is there any truth to the Tiger Mom or Stage Mom phenomenon?

◆ Our son was just identified as gifted. He's in the third grade. Already, the gifted coordinator at his high school is talking to us about grade acceleration, online courses, Honors and AP classes, and even dual enrollment at colleges for our son. We want to provide our son with a challenging and meaningful education, but don't want to overwhelm him. Any suggestions or cautionary notes?

◆ We've heard from other parents that the SENG Model Parent Groups[3] provide supportive, informational opportunities where parents can share concerns and learn more about giftedness. Would you recommend this type of support group for parents of the gifted?

◆ Okay, we realize that we have a gifted child. How do we know if we are setting unrealistically high goals and expectations for her?

◆ My wife and I fear that our daughter's accomplishments in school and with her violin and dance are becoming overly important to us. It's almost as if her accomplishments have become our own hopes and dreams. And we'd feel devastated if she doesn't live up to her potential. How can we regain our sanity and back off?

Suggested Resources

Chua, A. (2011). *Battle hymn of the tiger mother*. New York: Penguin Books.

Clarke-Fields, H. (2019). *Raising good humans: A mindful guide to breaking the cycle of reactive parenting and raising kind, confident kids*. Oakland, CA: New Harbinger Publications.

Daniels, S., & Piechowski, M. M. (Eds.) (2009). *Living with intensity*. Scottsdale, AZ: Great Potential Press.

Davidson Institute: www.davidsongifted.org

Davis, J. L. (2022). *Bright, black, and gifted: A guide for families of black gifted learners*. Oldham County, KY: Gifted Unlimited.

Delisle, J. (2006). *Parenting gifted kids: Tips for raising happy and successful children*. New York: Routledge.

Duckworth, A. (2016). *Grit: The power of passion and perseverance*. New York: Scribner.

Dweck, C. S. (2006). *Mindset: The new psychology of success*. New York: Random House.

Dyer, W. W. (2004). *The power of intention*. Carlsbad, CA: Hay House.

Gifted Homeschooler's Forum (GHF): https://ghflearners.org

Goleman, D. (2006). *Social intelligence: The new science of human relationships*. New York: Bantam Books.

Hoagies Gifted Education (Hoagies): www.hoagiesgifted.org

Hoagies' Gifted Kids & Teens: www.hoagieskids.org

Inman, T. F., & Kirchner, J. (2021). *Parenting gifted children 101: An introduction to gifted kids and their needs*. New York: Routledge.

Kabat-Zinn, J. (2018). *Meditation is not what you think*. New York: Hyperion.

Kennedy-Moore, E. (2011). *Smart parenting for smart kids*. New York: Jossey-Bass.

Kennedy-Moore, E. (2019). *Kid confidence*. Oakland, CA: New Harbinger Publications.

National Association for Gifted Children (NAGC): www.nagc.org

Nisbett, R. E. (2009). *Intelligence and how to get it*. New York: Norton.

Pfeiffer, S. I. (2003). Psychological considerations in raising a healthy gifted child. In P. Olszewski-Kubilius, L. Limburg-Weber, & S. I. Pfeiffer (Eds.). *Early gifts: Recognizing and nurturing children's talents* (pp. 173–185). Waco, TX: Prufrock Press.

Pfeiffer, S. I. (2013). *Serving the gifted*. New York: Routledge.

Rivero, L. (2010). *A parent's guide to gifted teens*. Scottsdale, AZ: Great Potential Press.

SENG Model Parent Groups (SMPG): www.sengifted.org and DeVries, A., & Webb, J. T. (2007). *Gifted parent groups: The SENG model*. Scottsdale, AZ: Great Potential Press.

Shapiro, L. E., & Holmes, J. (2008). *Let's be friends: A workbook to help kids learn social skills and make great friends*. Oakland, CA: New Harbinger Publications.

Shapiro, S., & White, C. (2014). *Mindful discipline*. Oakland, CA: New Harbinger Publications.

Siegel, D. J., & Haretzell, M. (2014). *Parenting from the inside out*. New York: Penguin Books.

Supporting Emotional Needs of the Gifted (SENG): www.sengifted.org

Tough, P. (2012). *How children succeed: Grit, curiosity, and the hidden power of character*. New York: Houghton Mifflin Harcourt Publishing Company.

Zakoian, C. (2020). *Raising gifted children*. Emeryville, CA: Rockridge Press.

Notes

1 The chapter appears in Olszewski-Kubilius, Limburg-Weber, & Pfeiffer (2003). *Early Gifts*; my book is titled: *Serving the Gifted*, by Steven Pfeiffer (2013). Both resources are listed at the end of this chapter.
2 Amu Chua's memoir about raising her highly talented children (2011).
3 See the book by DeVries, A., and Webb, J. T. (2007). *Gifted parent groups: The SENG model*. Scottsdale, AZ: Great Potential Press.

References

Baker, J. A. (1995). Depression and suicidal ideation among academically talented adolescents. *Gifted Child Quarterly, 39*, 218–223.

Carnegie, D. (1936; 1981 revised edition). *How to win friends and influence people*. New York: Simon & Schuster.

Cross, T. L. (2013). *Suicide among gifted children and adolescents: Understanding the suicidal mind*. Waco, TX: Prufrock Press.

Davidson, L., & Linnoila, M. (Eds.) (1991). *Risk factors for youth suicide*. New York: Hemisphere.

Davis, J. L. (2022). *Bright, black, and gifted: A guide for families of black gifted learners*. Oldham County, KY: Gifted Unlimited.

Hendin, H., & the Commission on Adolescent Suicide Prevention (2005). Youth suicide. In D. Evans, E. Foa, R. Gur, H. Hendin, C. O'Brien, M. Seligman, & B. Walsh (Eds.), *Treating and preventing adolescent mental health disorders: What we know and what we don't know* (pp. 431–495). Oxford: Oxford University Press.

Joiner, T. E. (2005). *Why people die by suicide*. Cambridge, MA: Harvard University Press.

Pfeiffer, S. I. (2013). *Serving the gifted*. New York: Routledge.

Pfeiffer, S. I., & Stocking, V. (2000). Vulnerabilities of academically gifted students. *Special Services in the Schools, 16*, 83–93.

8

Concluding Thoughts

Let me remind the reader of the quote cited at the very beginning of this pocketbook by famous psychiatrist, author, and Holocaust survivor Viktor Frankl, "When we are no longer able to change a situation, we are challenged to change ourselves" (1959).

One might ask, *"Aren't strengths of the heart really just an endearing but different name for social intelligence?"* This is a fair question to begin the final chapter. *Social intelligence* was a term first proposed over 100 years ago by Edward Thorndike, professor on the faculty at Teachers College, Columbia University. In a now-famous article that appeared in *Harper's Magazine* back in 1920, Professor Thorndike defined *social intelligence* as *the ability to understand and manage men and women and boys and girls, to act wisely in human relations.* In many ways, Thorndike's quaint definition of social intelligence is similar to what Howard Gardner calls *interpersonal intelligence*, one of his eight multiple intelligences (Gardner, 1983). The

DOI: 10.4324/9781003287070-8

term *social intelligence* also overlaps with science writer Daniel Goleman's description of *Emotional Intelligence*, which Goleman contends consists of self-awareness, self-regulation, motivation, empathy, and social skills (Goleman, 2007). *Social intelligence* also seems related to *theory of mind*, described earlier in this pocketbook. And it has an uncanny likeness to the colloquial term that I have repeatedly used, *street smarts*! Some clever readers might suggest that Edward Thorndike, Howard Gardner, Daniel Goleman, and I have all conspired to have woven different sweaters using essentially the same yarn! And perhaps the metaphor isn't entirely unwarranted.

When I first proposed the idea of *strengths of the heart*, I recognized that I wasn't proposing an original or groundbreaking new psychological theory. Rather, I was intertwining—weaving together to continue the knit sweater metaphor, a unified model using three well-established yarns—*Emotional Intelligence, social skills,* and *character strengths* (Pfeiffer, 2001, 2003; Pfeiffer & Blankenship, 2017). My own research and considerable anecdotal evidence suggest that when bright kids develop savvy and age-appropriate *social skills,* strong *Emotional Intelligence,* and keen *character strengths,* they are much more likely to successfully use their head strengths in smart ways to do well in life (Pfeiffer & Prado, 2022). They are much more likely to have positive mindsets, much more likely to be socially aware and able to take the perspective of others with different backgrounds and cultures, and much more prone to establish and maintain healthy and rewarding relationships, and be responsible decision-makers (Weissberg et al., 2015). This very point guided my passion for promoting *strengths of the heart*.

Part of my focus over the course of my career on *heart strengths* has been because of my concern over our culture's myopic obsession with IQ test scores, grades, class rankings, academic performance, and building fat résumés for our kids with the goal of getting them into elite, prestigious colleges (Borba, 2021). Somewhere along the way, we lost sight of the importance of developing the whole child. The head, heart, and soul of the gifted child! The academic clinician in me recognized that *social skills*, *Emotional Intelligence*, and *character strengths* are all necessary for even the smartest kids to optimize their human abilities and be resilient, compassionate, self-sufficient, and successful (Pfeiffer, 2017).

Parenting can often feel overwhelming. Especially for parents of special needs kids—kids who have disabilities, and kids who have special gifts and talents. Really, any child who is different from the norm presents unique challenges. And the more different or atypical from the norm, the greater the challenge! *"Am I handling things correctly? Am I doing the right thing? Am I messing up my gifted kid?"* Let's face it, parenting is a complicated adventure, full of unexpected, and unanticipated challenges. Especially for parents of kids who are different or special.

Of particular concern to me as a psychologist are those parents with a gifted child who is socially inept, not fitting in well, or has budding social-behavioral problems. Many well-meaning parents mistakenly wait without seeking professional help in the naïve hope for a sea change when their child gets older and matures. All-too-often, things don't improve for the bright child wanting in *heart strengths*. *Developmental decay theory* suggests that early social-emotional problems left untreated can fester and lead to more serious psychological problems (Pfeiffer, 2013; Post, 2022). All the more reason for parents to encourage *strengths of the heart* from an early age. Encouraging *heart strengths* is every bit as important to your child's success as attending to their *head strengths*.

Recall that I included a chapter specifically on the importance of taking care of yourself if you hope to successfully parent your gifted child. This is such an important point—why I mention it again now, in the closing chapter. In my 40 years' experience as a family therapist, clinical psychologist, and parent educator, I have come to recognize that it is almost impossible to teach social-emotional skills if you, as a parent, don't have your own act together psychologically. If you are the kind of adult who doesn't have strong *heart strengths*—those important soft, people skills, then it will be darn difficult teaching your gifted child about *Emotional Intelligence, character strengths* and *social skills*.

As a parent of a gifted child, you can be socially inept—clueless in terms of people skills or street smarts, and yet successfully teach your bright child trigonometry or calculus, astrophysics, nanotechnology, hermeneutics, 19th century occultism, astrology, Shakespeare, Milton, microbiology, quantum physics, organic chemistry, or Confucian philosophy! This is true. If you have the content expertise, you can pull it off without being socially savvy. I've seen many very bright but otherwise socially bungling parents teach their gifted kids' esoteric subject matter. No problem at all! But you can't teach *strengths of the heart* if you are socially clumsy and not savvy with people skills. It just doesn't work well. So please don't neglect the lessons found in Chapter 2.

Concluding Comments

It is always hard to end a book. This is certainly true for me. It is like saying a final farewell to a client that I have come to care a lot about. I close the chapter by offering a *Baker's Dozen Tips*. This is how I typically conclude my last parent counseling sessions—with the gift of a few parting parenting tips. Some of these tips you will recall I have already mentioned in this pocketbook. Some are ideas that appear in my other books. And others are tips that I borrowed from respected colleagues. I hope that you find these dozen-or-so tips useful in your continuing journey parenting your gifted child.

1. Accept That Your Child Is Different

Every child is unique. No two kids are the same, even siblings or twins growing up in the same family! Kids who are gifted and talented are different in many ways from their nongifted peers and their siblings. They have special needs that oftentimes challenge and confuse their teachers, peers, babysitter, coaches, and tutors. You probably already realize that your gifted child is different. This can put an added burden on you and on your spouse, family, and friends to understand, support, and value your gifted child's distinctive learning and social-emotional needs, struggles to fit in, and oftentimes asynchronous development, overexcitabilities, greater emotional reactivity, multipotentiality, and quirky behaviors. And passion.

2. Become an Expert on Giftedness and Gifted Education

Reading self-help books like this one is crucial to help you learn as much as you can about giftedness and exceptionalities. For many years, I taught a popular course entitled *The psychology of giftedness and talent development* on the campus of Florida State University. My most engaged and passionate students were parents of gifted kids! They taught me that they benefited immeasurably from readings, websites, podcasts, attending college classes, and gifted conferences and parent workshops offered by organizations such as NAGC and SENG. Become an expert about giftedness, individual differences, gifted education, ability grouping, talent development, acceleration, honors and AP classes, home schooling, specialized schools for the gifted, dual enrollment at colleges, twice exceptionalities, and the unique social-emotional needs of exceptional kids. Your expertise will serve you well advocating for your gifted child. *Hint: Check out the resources listed following each chapter.*

3. Learn to Advocate for Your Child

You didn't bargain for or expect to become your child's advocate when you were pregnant! But taking on the role of child advocate and ambassador for your child quickly becomes an important, sometimes essential, and weighty responsibility. Most adults in your child's life have very little understanding of giftedness. Many view gifted kids as a low priority who can easily make it on their own without any special resources or programs. Many view parents of the gifted as pushy. You may find yourself needing to educate, inform, and correct misperceptions and myths about the gifted. *Hint: Advocate in a tactful, gentle but self-assured and knowledgeable way.* You may find it necessary to educate your child's teachers, principal, school board members, pediatrician, coaches, tutors, and even Sunday School and religious leader! Advocacy can sometimes become exhausting and uncomfortably conflictual. You will need to learn when and with whom to pick your battles, when to back off, and how to graciously and gracefully compromise.

4. Pick Your Battles and Don't Sweat the Small Stuff

Advocating for your child is a very tricky business. I often hold consulting sessions with frustrated and angry parents who perceive their child's teacher or school as obstinate, unbending, and stubborn. At times, the battles appear unwinnable. Even when the parent is justified in advocating for their special-needs child. All too often, schools misunderstand, misinterpret, or ignore federal, state, or school district special education laws, rules, and regulations that impact the gifted student. There are some battles too important not to fight. There are some battles that are unwinnable. And there are many small, annoying things that are best to let go and not sweat.

5. Encourage Your Child's Strengths

Every gifted child is born with a unique array or profile of abilities. For example, some kids display, at a very young age, uncanny reading or language ability. Other gifted kids surprise us, at a very early age, with almost supernatural theatrical talent or musical, artistic, gymnastic, mathematical, athletic, or spatial ability. The range of potential gifts is limited only by what society values (Pfeiffer, 2015). And many bright kids possess multiple gifts. Of course, the environment plays a crucial role in the development and unfolding of these embryonic, promising abilities first observed at an early age. It's never a simple nature *vs.* nurture matter. From almost birth, there's an intimate, ongoing, and synergistic interplay between God-given gifts and the availability of a nurturing family to encourage and foster these nascent gifts. The tip here is to be observant of your child's natural or innate abilities and support them. A still-classic and often-cited study by Bloom (1985) confirms that young, world-class achievers don't reach the highest levels of accomplishment without family support.

6. Celebrate Persistence and Grit

Several researchers have confirmed that kids thrive when they are encouraged from an early age to work hard, learn to enjoy difficult and challenging tasks, and not give up when the going gets tough. Parents should set positive, realistic but reasonably high expectations for performance. Gifted kids thrive when parents (and teachers) focus on the effort expended and not as much on the outcome or grade. This focus on the process and effort builds a positive mindset. Mistakes, failures, and disappointments as part of the process should be encouraged and valued. Gifted kids, like all kids, prefer schoolwork that is appropriately challenging intellectually and, also, personally meaningful. But kids need to learn to graciously accept that not all assignments, projects, or training regimes are going to be fun, appealing, or consequential. Parents play a key role in helping their gifted child to accept this important life lesson.

7. Promote and Embrace Balance

I already offered the tip of encouraging your gifted child's unique strengths. At the same time, you need to protect yourself from getting too caught up in focusing exclusively on your child's gifts or special talents to the neglect of other important social, developmental, spiritual, or community experiences. It is tempting to provide your gifted child with almost every available opportunity, experience, and resource. Yes—helping to nurture and develop your gifted child's talent or special ability is an important parental task! However, when the scales tip and you find yourself placing excessive emphasis—in terms of time, family financial resources, mental energy, travel, rearranged schedules, sacrifices to other children and your spouse—on promoting the special talent, both the gifted child and the family can suffer by missing out on important socialization experiences. This can actually put you, your gifted child, and the family at risk for psychological problems. Balance is the guiding principle here. In my book *Serving the Gifted* (2015), I provide examples from my clinical work when the scales tip too far toward imbalance.

8. Don't Shy Away from Discipline and Setting Rules and Limits

Clearly stated parental expectations and family discipline, rules, and limits for conduct are crucial for all kids, gifted kids, and not-gifted kids alike. Helping your gifted child to understand and respect rules within the home helps them to understand and respect rules within the school and neighborhood. It is almost impossible for a gifted child to grow up in today's complex, multicultural, and diverse society and become successful, worthwhile, and resilient and not accept society's rules. When your child learns to follow family rules and limits, and respect discipline, they are acquiring foundational social skills on how to get along with others, maintain friendships, deal with conflict and disagreement, control their emotions, and recognize that they are part of a much larger social world. Family rules and appropriate limits communicate a sense of security and the message of parental love. To my surprise and disappointment, some authorities in the gifted field suggest that gifted kids need fewer constraints or limits than others (Webb, Gore, & Amend, 2007). There is absolutely no research supporting this proposition. As a parent, it is tempting and even seductive to think that your gifted child has better judgement and is more socially mature or more emotionally intelligent than other kids her or his age. Not true! *Advice: Parents: don't shy away from discipline, rules, and limits in the home!*

9. Create a Culture of Striving and Excellence

A close relative to the tip of celebrating persistence and grit is the recommendation to encourage the family value of striving for excellence. I am not suggesting an excessive focus and unrealistic expectations on obtaining the highest grades and perfect performance. That is not helpful. It can push any child, including gifted kids, over the edge between healthy striving for excellence and unhealthy perfectionism. Excessive emphasis on performance—in academics, athletics, the arts, or really any field or domain, can create debilitating anxiety, dread, and fear of failure, rather than what we are aiming for—joy, spontaneity, passion, self-discipline, creativity, and a love of learning.

I worked with a highly gifted young gymnast, ranked among the top three female gymnasts in her age group nationally. Her parents consulted me because their young, gifted daughter had recently, in their words, "simply refused to practice floor and balance beam exercises that she needed to learn if she was to continue to compete at a national level." Counseling this young athlete and her well-meaning but highly competitive and pushy parents revealed that the unrelenting pressure to perform perfectly and best at all competitions had created a paralyzing dynamic for their talented daughter. Her parents' constant encouragement, indefatigable tips, and unrelenting feedback before and after each practice reached a point where all their daughter heard was criticism and disapproval. Counseling helped the parents to step back and relinquish their self-appointed role as unofficial coach and take on a less involved but more enjoyable parental role.

Family values that support and encourage hard work, persistence, enjoying challenges, never giving up, and being intellectually curious and creative all convey vital and powerful messages to the gifted child that establish attitudes and beliefs consistent with pursuing lofty goals and developing one's potential (Pfeiffer, 2013). For example, exposing your gifted child to a variety of intellectual and cultural activities, encouraging hobbies and recreational pursuits, setting high expectations for performance, and modeling behaviors that reflect scholarly, intellectual, and creative activities send a clear message that your child is likely to internalize.

10. Avoid Being an Overly Competitive or Pushy Parent

You've probably heard about or even know a parent who is living through their gifted or talented child. They are way too emotionally attached to their gifted child and absorbed by her accomplishments. This is the stereotypical *"tiger mother"* or *"stage mom."* I observed this from the sidelines during the time when our now adult daughter was a much-heralded young soccer player. At the young age of ten, our daughter successfully competed for a spot on the highly select women's Olympic Development Soccer Program (ODP), a feeder for the USA soccer team. As a parent, traveling with my young daughter to ODP women's team practices and events, I saw a few fellow parents pathologically preoccupied, spellbound, and riveted by their own young daughter's athletic prowess on the turf. They had lost all perspective on social graces and what an appropriate role model as parent should be. They were *over-the-top*, living through their gifted child's athletic accomplishments. They would stealthily treat the head coach to meals or give the assistant coaches small gifts as a furtive way to endear their daughter's playing time on the field. Ultimately, their extreme overinvolvement and pushy ways created a disturbing and traumatic toll for their daughter. This reckless behavior by overinvolved tiger mothers occurs on the sidelines of playing fields, stages, art studios, classrooms, labs, and really any setting where gifted kids are developing their special talents. I once had to deal with a heedless, excessively pushy, and interfering parent of one of my doctoral students! The father's interference was annoying, for sure. But I was more concerned about his impact on his bright and accomplished daughter's ego.

11. Remember That no School or Gifted Program Is Ideal

Author Gail Post (2022) aptly reminds parents that no public, private, charter, boarding, or even homeschool setting is perfect. No one school will meet all your gifted child's academic, social, emotional, and spiritual needs. You will quickly become disappointed if you hold out the unrealistic expectation that there exists the one perfect school for your gifted child. Following the Covid-19 crisis, I now often consult with parents of gifted kids virtually. The video conferencing platform Zoom has allowed dozens of parents from across the globe to easily afford a virtual consultation without the cost of a flight and hotel to meet me in person. All-too-often, parents have contacted me on Zoom seeking a recommendation for the one ideal school for their gifted child. And all-too-often, they are disappointed when I explain that there are many good schools and programs for the gifted, across the globe, but each option undoubtedly requires compromises on their part. There is no perfect school for the gifted. There are always trade-offs among top schools, just as there are in life!

12. Don't Neglect Your Child's Social-emotional Needs

The focus of this pocketbook, of course, has been on this one tip! By now, you are an authority on recognizing the importance of *not* neglecting the social-emotional development of your gifted child. When gifted kids have savoir-faire with age-appropriate *social skills*, perceptive knowhow applying *Emotional Intelligence*, and strong and steely *character strengths*, they are much more likely to use their strong head strengths in smart ways to do well in life. They will be much more likely to have positive mindsets. They will be much more likely to be socially aware and able to take the perspective of others with different backgrounds and cultures. They will be much more prone to establish and maintain healthy and rewarding relationships. And they will be much more likely to make responsible decisions and successfully cope with life's many challenges. *Helpful tip: Strengths of the heart are important in your gifted child's life.*

13. Finally, Take Care of Yourself: Self-care Matters!

The final tip that concludes this chapter is familiar to you by now! You probably recall that I encourage you to take care of yourself so that you can optimize raising kind, compassionate, caring, resilient, emotionally intelligent, well-adjusted bright kids. I encourage you to reduce the level of stress in your life, practice self-compassion and self-kindness, and learn how to keep your cool and model calm behavior for your gifted child. I encourage you to try to let the little things go, identify, and then disarm your personal triggers, and create a peaceful home life—including regular family meetings. Finally, I encourage you embrace self-care by eating healthy, getting enough sleep, and exercising regularly. All these self-care remedies work. But none are easy to put into action, of course. But then, nothing that is important is easy. I wish you much success!

Suggested Resources

Borba, M. (2022). *Thrivers: The surprising reasons why some kids struggle and others shine*. New York: Penguin Random House.

Carnegie, D. (1937). *How to win friends and influence people* (11th printing). New York: Simon and Schuster.

Clarke-Fields, H. (2019). *Raising good humans: A mindful guide to breaking the cycle of reactive parenting and raising kind, confident kids*. Oakland, CA: New Harbinger Publications.

Davis, J. L. (2022). *Bright, black, and gifted: A guide for families of black gifted learners*. Oldham County, KY: Gifted Unlimited.

Doucleff, M. (2021). *Hunt, gather, parent: What ancient cultures can teach us about the lost art of raising happy, helpful little humans*. New York: Simon & Schuster.

Johnson-Dias, J. (2021). *Parent like it matters: How to raise joyful, change-making girls*. New York: Ballantine Books.

Kennedy-Moore, E. (2019). *Kid confidence: Help your child make friends, build resilience, and develop real self-esteem*. Oakland, CA: New Harbinger Publications.

Leman, K. (2021). *Raising successful kids*. Ada, MI: Revell Books.

Pfeiffer, S. I. (2003). Psychological considerations in raising a healthy gifted child. In P. Olszewski-Kubilius, L. Limburg-Weber, & S. I. Pfeiffer (Eds.). *Early gifts: Recognizing and nurturing children's talents* (pp. 173–185). Waco, TX: Prufrock Press.

Rivero, L. (2010). *A parent's guide to gifted teens*. Scottsdale, AZ: Great Potential Press.

Siegel, D. J., & Payne Bryson, T. (2011). *The whole-brain child*. New York: Bantam Books.

Unell, B. C., & Wyckoff, J. L. (1995). *20 Teachable virtues: Practical ways to pass on lessons of virtue and character to your children*. New York: A Pedigree Book.

Warner, M. & Coursey, C. M. (2021). *The 4 habits of raising joy-filled kids*. New York: Northfield Publishing Group.

Zaki, J. (2019). *The war for kindness: Building empathy in a fractured world*. New York: Crown.

References

Bloom, B. S. (Ed.) (1985). *Developing talent in young people*. New York: Ballentine Books.

Borba, M. (2021). *Thrivers: The surprising reasons why some kids struggle and others shine*. New York: Putnam.

Coleman, D. (2007). *Social intelligence*. New York: Bantam Books.

Cross, T. L. (2013). *Suicide among gifted children and adolescents: Understanding the suicidal mind.* Waco, TX: Prufrock Press.

Davis, J. L. (2022). *Bright, black, and gifted: A guide for families of black gifted learners.* Oldham County, KY: Gifted Unlimited.

Frankl, V. (1959). Man's search for meaning. Boston, MA: Beacon Press.

Gardner, H. (1983). *Frames of mind: The theory of multiple intelligences.* New York: Basic Books.

Pfeiffer, S. I. (2001). Emotional intelligence: Popular but elusive construct. *Roeper Review, 23*, 138–142.

Pfeiffer, S. I. (2003). Psychological considerations in raising a healthy gifted child. In P. Olszewski-Kubilius, L. Limburg-Weber, & S. I. Pfeiffer (Eds.). *Early gifts: Recognizing and nurturing children's talents* (pp. 173–185). Waco, TX: Prufrock Press.

Pfeiffer, S. I. (2013). *Serving the gifted.* New York: Routledge.

Pfeiffer, S. I. (2015). *Essentials of gifted assessment.* Hoboken, NJ: Wiley.

Pfeiffer, S. I. (2017). Success in the classroom and in life: Focusing on strengths of the head and strengths of the heart. *Gifted Education International, 33*, 95–101.

Pfeiffer, S. I., & Blankenship, A. P. (2017). Lessons learned from working with highly gifted and creative kids. *Psychology and Education, 54*, 24–32.

Post, G. (2022). *The gifted parenting journey.* Goshen, KY: Gifted Unlimited.

Webb, J. T., Gore, J. L., & Amend, E. R. (2007). *A parent's guide to gifted children.* Scottsdale, AZ: Great Potential Press.

Weissberg, R. P., Durlak, J. A., Domitrovich, C. E., & Gullotta, T. P. (2015). Social and emotional learning: Past, present, and future. In J. A. Durlak, C. E. Domitrovich, R. P. Weissberg, & T. P. Gullotta (Eds.), *Handbook of social and emotional learning. Research and Practice* (pp. 3–19). New York: Guilford Press.

Printed in the United States
by Baker & Taylor Publisher Services